Successful Bonsai Growing

Successful Bonsai Growing

Peter Adams

WARD LOCK LIMITED·LONDON

First published in Great Britain in 1978 by
Ward Lock Limited, 82 Gower Street,
London WC1E 6EQ, a Pentos Company.

Reprinted 1979, 1981, 1982

House editor Teresa Mozley
Text filmset in Times by
Rembrandt Filmsetting Ltd Watford

Printed and bound in Hong Kong by
South China Printing Co.

British Library Cataloguing in Publication Data

Adams, P
    Successful bonsai
    1. Bonsai
I. Title
635.9'77   SB435.5

ISBN 0-7063-5376-5-Pbk
ISBN 0-7063-5373-0

Contents

Introduction 7

1 The Basic Styles 7

2 How to Develop the Styles 14

3 Raising Bonsai from Seedlings 29

4 Cuttings 42

5 Layering and Grafting 44

6 Nursery Stock 46

7 Collecting Natural Trees 49

8 The Bonsai Process 53

9 Soil 67

10 Pots and Containers 68

11 Watering 69

12 Feeding 72

13 Placement 73

14 Diseases 74

15 Pests 77

16 Tools 78

17 Bonsai Data 78

18 Conclusion 99

Index 101

ACKNOWLEDGEMENT

I am indebted to Dan Barton for all the photographic work. It should be pointed out that all photographs were taken in the nursery inside greenhouses, and not under studio conditions.

P.D.A.

INTRODUCTION

Bonsai as we know it today is the culmination of a process that has been evolving in Japan from the twelfth century and even earlier in China.

By definition, a Bonsai is a forest tree in a pot. The tree is small and kept small by regular pruning techniques. It is above all, a healthy and happy plant. It is not a genetic dwarf (where in nature, growth would be negligible each year) but the outcome of a cycle of mechanical dwarfing.

Nature itself can apply these mechanical techniques to a plant in the forms of extreme weathers, poor soil and so on, thus producing natural Bonsai or dwarfed trees. These are not confined to Japan but may be found anywhere in the world.

A natural tree, the product of the natural dwarfing described, is always a superior article and usually has a well-tapered trunk as a result of checked growth each season. Such trees are eagerly sought for and valued throughout the world by Bonsai fanciers. The old natural trees provided the initial inspiration in China and Japan.

The aims of this book are to clarify Bonsai for the newcomer and perhaps to suggest a few techniques that can produce a nice tree quickly. If I succeed in either respect I shall be very pleased.

1 THE BASIC STYLES

As the diversity of shapes is so amazing, there exists a standard style index aimed at simplifying shape selection in training. This is based on forms best suited to the species.

Upright Single Trunk
Usually a formal style and based on well-grown specimen trees in perfect conditions. The overall form is conical, branching is tiered and the trunk is tapered and vertical.

LARCH, CYPRESS, PINE, CRYPTOMERIA, SPRUCE, FIR, YEW, CEDAR, ZELKOVA, ELM, and TRIDENT MAPLE are among the best trees for the Upright style. This style calls for a neat textured variety, as the trunk and main branch lines are very obvious. There are several classical arrangements of branching in the tiered upright style. The main style by branch disposition is: the first major lower limb left or right (never twin or opposite branched); the second branch higher up on the opposing side and the third branch to the rear. The rear branch will often sweep down and appear to be between 1 and 2. The fourth branch follows the first, left or right. The fifth follows the second. The sixth is arranged between 1st and 3rd. The residue of smaller branches to the apex are trained to conform to the conical form, and may be placed according to taste, providing the cone is preserved.

The intervals between branches are important. The lowest interval from root to first branch sets the style and thereafter the intervals should get narrower progressively to the apex. Branch lengths should diminish also, so the first branch may legitimately be long and heavy, to reinforce the cone shape. Branches should be varied in length for interest.

The arrangement of branch planes in the formal style is rigidly horizontal or slightly downswept. They are arranged radially around the trunk so no neighbouring foliage mass overlaps another.

A typical radial arrangement may be: No 1 lower branch 9 o'clock; No 2 higher at 3.30 o'clock; No 3 at 1 o'clock; No 4 at 8 o'clock; No 5 at 2 o'clock; No 6 at 10.30. These positions read from dead overhead trunk centre.

BESOM

This as the name implies looks like an upturned broom. It is the style that evokes the winter shape of elms and oaks and to most people 'looks like a tree'.

ELM, ZELKOVA, OAK, BIRCH are the most widely grown in this style. The deployment of branches is varied and these may start classically at one third of the way up the trunk, sweeping upwards into a diverse and multi-leadered tree with a domed head.

Other variants are the Besom with the leader intact, so the trunk has a slow taper, flanked with fanning branches; the very tall style, often with a twin trunk; or, the very low style, where the spread is much greater than the height.

8

Root formation in this style is of the highest importance, as a surfaced, radial system greatly enhances the natural feeling. The way to achieve this is fully dealt with later.

INFORMAL UPRIGHT
In this style the trunk moves from the vertical about 10°–15°, generally curving three-dimensionally in one or more gentle S-configurations. It is a very graceful style and has universal appeal. It is based on the changing trunk line of trees where natural causes bring realignments in trunk growth.

ELM, MAPLE, BEECH, HORNBEAM, BIRCH, HACKBERRY, CRAB APPLE, APRICOT, QUINCE, JASMINE, AZALEA, COTONEASTER, FIRETHORN, PINE and JUNIPER are all commonly seen trained in this way.

Trunk and branches are arranged in contra-relation. Where the trunk curves, a branch is selected on the outer side of the bend and this is curved in a gentle sweep, away from the bend. Branch masses are assymetrical, and balance is achieved by a broadly triangular form with the trunk in counterpoise.

Root formation is again important and the radial system is favoured.

LEANING AND WINDSWEPT
The trunk is often at 30° plus and may be curved or straight. It is based on trees taking root in adverse environments where either subsidence or weather sculpts the sapling tree.

ELM, MAPLE, BEECH, HORNBEAM, HAWTHORN, CRAB APPLE, APRICOT, QUINCE, AZALEA, COTONEASTER, WISTERIA, PINE and JUNIPER all make very good subjects.

The root system is of great importance, providing a visual anchor. A claw shape looks very well. With the leaning trunk, the secret is to provide balance by raking back branch lines. If lower limbs on the outer angle sweep back over the trunk base, and those on the inner angle are kept shorter, stability is easily achieved—both visual and practical.

The windswept is very much akin, except that most branches sweep away from the trunk rake on the inner angle. The effect is like a pennant held at an angle in a stiff breeze. Branches on the outer angle should be kept short. A little study of trees along the coast will suggest all sorts of exciting possibilities.

9

CASCADE AND SEMI-CASCADE

The trunk falls away over the pot rim in a gentle sweep in the semi-cascade, or plunges vertically down in the full cascade. This is a higly decorative style seen most often in mountainous country or on cliffs. Trees like this are not very common in the United Kingdom although they do exist.

MAPLE, CRAB APPLE, HAWTHORN, QUINCE, AZALEA, COTONEASTER, WISTERIA, PINE and JUNIPER are widely appreciated and it is a good style for any naturally weeping species such as WILLOW or LABURNUM.

The prime rule is to use a deep pot to display the form to advantage and give visual/physical stability. Trunk patterns are varied, but with the Cascade, the trunk curves over the rim and the first branch is trained inwards to soften the line of the pot. The trunk then moves outwards and downwards in a series of diminishing curves, with successive branches arranged on the outer bends. Branches are kept cleanly pruned beneath and an impression of floating results, like clouds.

With the semi-cascade, between trunk base and pot rim as the trunk curves over, there is usually a vertical head of foliage that balances the lower masses. This appears as the apex of the tree although in reality it is the base branch. The true trunk carries on in a downward curve that usually tilts up again at the tip. Foliage masses are arranged either side of the trunk, but a neater appearance results where they are in alignment with, or slightly above the trunk.

Roots should be clearly defined and dominant on the outer angle.

The full cascade should be displayed on a high stand to prevent branch damage.

CLASPED TO STONE

Again, a mountain tree style or one that may occur where a seedling takes root in walling or amongst rocks.

MAPLE, AZALEA, COTONEASTER, JASMINE, QUINCE, PINE, JUNIPER and CYPRESS make graceful arrangements.

There are two main divisions of this style: the tree or trees that sit in a saddle on a rock with roots arranged in fissures down the rock wall to soil beneath; or the style where the tree is confined purely to the stone and they become one unit.

Both styles are extremely attractive. Some standard arrangements include: a tall rock with tree or trees planted vertically in a formal arrangement so a mountain giant, or grove, is suggested; a medium depth stone with a single tree or trees with heavy downswept lower limbs reminiscent of the semi-cascade; a flattish rock with a single tree or trees gripping the stone with an aged root system, and the flat stone with a cluster or grove sitting on a mound of soil.

Trees with the right stones quickly give satisfying results. The 'right' stones are those medium to dark in colour with an interesting texture. Though light in colour, Tufa rock from Wales and Derbyshire often has a fascinating form. Beware of planting Azaleas on Tufa as the lime content can kill. Apart from Tufa, which is soft, the right stone should be hard enough to resist erosion. Never use rocks straight from the sea-shore—always soak them in several changes of water, probably for a year, to neutralize the salt content. The final touch is the planting of the unit in a flattish pot. The pot should be a long one to give visual stability.

GROUPS
Twin Trunk
Often called Mother and Child, are simple to arrange and give a charming result. Forks should be as low down the trunk as possible and trunks should be fairly close. If a nice example is found with the fork too far up the trunk, consider layering below the division. There is a section on layering later.

One trunk should dominate both in caliper (trunk thickness) and in height. If an example is found with both trunks of equal caliper, try drastically thinning the foliage on one and allowing the other full rein for a couple of years. Usually the heavily foliaged trunk will thicken up satisfactorily.

Branch planes should project outwards in alternating tiers radially around both trunks and arrangements should always be considered as a unit when pruning, grooming or wiring. Relating the twin verticals and the branches as assymetrical shapes is fascinating, and Scots Pine clusters for example seen on a hillside will often give ideas for something really original. Actual trunk form may be curved or straight.

Triple Trunk

These are treated in the same way, but caliper differences are even more important. If an example is found with the correct balance of thick to thin caliper, then further possibilities open up for depth in the shape. If the main trunk is displayed in front, with the second and third trunks seen moving away diagonally, an added dimension of perspective is created. If at the same time the foliage mass diminishes, the feeling of distance is still further enhanced.

Four trunks are not used in Bonsai, or even numbers generally, with the exception of two. The reasons are partly based on Japanese philosophy that believes odd numbers represent immortality, but more practically because odd numbers are easier to arrange.

Five and Seven Trunk

These are variations treated in the same way, but less importance is attached to caliper, provided that there is at least one major trunk. All the above may be created by layering, or by cutting young trees off at the soil level so that a coppice is created.

Clump

This is the variant where there are many sprouts (often fifteen and more) growing out from the same area at the soil line. The thinning out and arrangement should aim at producing the overall triangle of foliage, sitting like a cap on diverse trunks which are spaced at closer or wider intervals, so that an impression of a grove is created. If frontal placement is open and the back closer, the illusion is heightened. Foliage, too, if lower at the back helps the effect.

Those trunks at the right and left should have their out-facing branches encouraged by removal or shortening of the inner ones. Centrally placed trunks should have their lower limbs removed and their top branches arranged toward front and back. This is the standard method for group branch arrangement and it obviates branch entanglement and line confusion. Those removed include also the areas that all trees will shed naturally through lack of light when planted closely together, so do it initially and help the Bonsai.

Groups

These normally comprise nine trees or above although smaller numbers are popular. The arrangements are made with the major tree to the front, flanked by two trees of lesser height and caliper, slightly to the rear, left and right of the main tree. The main tree is planted at $\frac{1}{3}$ from the left or right hand edge of the group. The rest of the trees are then set around this triangular nucleus in order of height and caliper. Small and low-branched trees are planted to the rear. Care should be taken to vary the intervals, or negative areas, between trunks to avoid monotony. Providing no tree overlaps completely when viewed from the front or side, and that the nucleus principle is followed, the placement of the trees in terms of negative areas is fluid. Do try for variety in these areas. Groups give immediately enjoyable results and get better every year.

Raft Style

Another group variant, where the trunk of some easy-rooting species is laid horizontally—said to represent a raft—and branches trained up become 'trees'. After some years a very attractive, bulky-based forest results. The main trunk will send out roots along its length which may be surfaced and so add charm. This is a man-made style.

Root Connected

Similar in appearance to the raft, which it inspired, this is a naturally occurring phenomenon. A freely-suckering species will be damaged, even to the extent where the main trunk dies, but sprouts appear all along major surfaced roots and round the trunk base.

When transferred to Bonsai scale, the sight of trunks rising from interlocking roots is very effective: ELM, WILLOW and CRAB APPLE are good.

The 'trees' should be arranged on the standard group principle.

2   HOW TO DEVELOP THE STYLES

UPRIGHT SINGLE TRUNK
These are formed from straight-trunked seedlings or by
layering suitably shaped tips of mature plants. Root flair from
the trunk at the soil line and the radial spread of surfaced roots
are most important. A layering gives one the optimum chance
of programming this, otherwise careful searching with the
fingers will establish the presence of these with seedlings or
nursery stock. If either of the latter have three or more good
strong surface roots, then they may be chosen, as additional
roots may be formed by drilling through to the heartwood at
ground level, inserting a dab of hormone rooting powder in the
hole and then mounding a little moistened peat/sand mixture
round the wound. A root will appear in the area within a month
or two.

A good trunk taper is the major consideration with dense
foliage and the recommended species will feature this in most
cases.

As stated, the lower branches are the longest and should be
well placed in relation to the root, left or right with branching
as described to the apex. This means a lot of initial thinning so
consider the tree carefully before selection and try to imagine it
bulk-reduced. Branch frequency, giving multi-choice at pruning time is therefore the third consideration.

Whatever the source, prune unwanted branches and establish the plant for a season in a temporary container large
enough to accept the root mass without trimming. Surface the
major base roots and spread them with the fingers and then
concentrate on growing a healthy tree for the year. Feed and
water well.

When branch pruning, leave snags behind as they can often be
utilized as design features (fully discussed under Pruning).
After selection for decoration, remove excess snags.

During the following season, further shaping is carried out
on the established tree and this time careful attention is paid to
the appearance of each branch plane.

Clean out hanging foliage that breaks the horizontal branch
line and any foliage clinging close into the trunk. With scissors,

create a roughly triangular form over the whole tree. Arrange each branch with wire so that the major line is horizontal or slightly downswept. Wire every sub-branch in herringbone formation and bend to conform to the main branch contour. One thus creates a pad of foliage sitting along the main limb. Further refine each pad with scissors so that the contour is smooth and then arrange the branches like radiating spokes so that each receives its share of light. Feed and water the tree well after styling and finger-prune wayward shoots, but allow the tree to be a little hairy in this first year. You can always neaten in the following spring with scissors. Further refinement of the shape in ensuing seasons and of course the transfer to the final pot is all that is necessary to create the basic style.

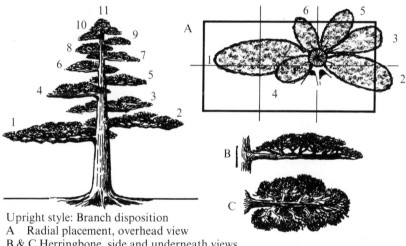

Upright style: Branch disposition
A   Radial placement, overhead view
B & C Herringbone, side and underneath views

BESOM

Popularly these are best started from seed, but cuttings and layering propagations provide excellent alternatives. Rarely, nursery stock will yield good results, but as this normally entails heavy trunk chopping, these trees will be inferior. Most rare of all are the naturally occurring small Besom trees which can be collected from the wild. These do exist, and there are superb examples of Myrtle for instance to be found in Wales.

Normally, as rootage is so vital, only those examples with the full 360° surface systems are chosen. These must be carefully established for a year, with even more than average care and attention paid to surface-root distribution. In the first year, vertical support should be given to ensure a straight trunk before, say, the 25cm/10in point is reached.

In the following season, where plants of Zelkova are used light wire should be applied to emerging branches. The other species recommended take care of themselves regarding upward sweep and need only be straightened with wire. The decision as to style of Besom must be taken now. If the undivided, tapered trunk style is favoured, allow the terminal shoot to develop but watch the watering and place the tree in a well ventilated, sunny position. If water is not too generously given, in conjunction with the new placement the terminal will develop slowly and the trunk will assume taper. The lateral buds in favoured positions should be encouraged by removing all others by rubbing off with the fingers. Branching with all Besoms should be widely spaced near the base, with progressively narrower intervals between till the head is reached which divides diffusely.

With the classically proportioned Besom, the trunk may be pinched out or pruned at a height of 20cm/8in or less. Ensuing branch growth will radiate and ramify outwards in a 'Busby' form to the desired height. Branch directions may be arranged with light wiring and in such a manner that no crossing of main limbs occurs. Sub-branching should not begin too close in to the trunk, but should increase in ramification towards the

Besom style: Classic variant

Tapered trunk variant

contour edge. A feeling of upturned umbrella spokes is the ideal framework. Finger pinching of evolving branches at one third of their desired spread will create the right effect. Study the negative areas (like windows) between main limbs and try to vary them so a naturally diverse system results.

The Low Besom style follows the same lines but the initial pinch may be as low as 10cm/4in in height. Ensuing branch growth should be encouraged sideways and the top therefore firmly dealt with to gain the spread.

The Besom should be transplanted every two years back into the temporary container until such time as the form is distinct. Premature potting, particularly of Zelkova, inhibits trunk fattening.

INFORMAL STYLE

This style may be developed from a collected tree, nursery stock or any of the propagation stock material. The accent is on graceful posture and great care should be taken in material selection. When pre-formed trees are considered, such as the collected article or nursery stock, select only those that will not need heavy trunk chopping in styling.

The initial establishment period should see the tree planted at an angle of 10°–15° left or right, with the surface roots raised to complement the trunk base. Those trees without existing trunk curve features should be trained in the following season with any variant of the wiring techniques. A typical arrange-

Besom style: Twin trunk variant

Low spreading variant

17

ment would be to take the trunk either left or right in a natural bend to the first lower limb. This is done in such a manner as to leave the branch on the outside of the bend. The trunk should then be brought back in contra-relation so the second limb appears on the outer bend. The second bend and subsequent trunk changes should lessen towards the apex. The whole tree should then be inclined back away from the base to the midway point on the trunk and the top half should be brought forward. This simple technique gives satisfying depth to the design, particularly if the third branch to the rear can be glimpsed more or less at the change of plane point.

Arrange the main branches in downward sweeps away from the trunk. The trunk/branch axis should be seen clearly in lower branching but may be masked higher up. The style is discussed in some detail in the chapter on Seedlings.

LEANING AND WINDSWEPT

Collected or nursery stock are recommended, as to be convincing both these styles need a tapered trunk of some age. Moorland country will often provide excellent material. Look particularly for Scots Pine.

Once established, the leaning style must have the lower limbs on the outer angle greatly encouraged by feeding. They should be arranged with wire to gives a series of stepped tiers. The lowest should curve over the trunk base and away from the

Informal style:
Front view

Side view, front facing left. Trunk swings back to midway point then head comes forward inclined direction to some distance. Subsequent branch lengths then diminish towards the apex which itself may be raked to point slightly down towards the first limb. The limbs on the inner angle should also be stepped, but kept shorter, to create an overall triangle. Each branch plane should be horizontally arranged in a herringbone to conform to the step, using wire and scissors. This style and the Windswept will appear elegant if foliage masses are kept to a minimum. Particular attention should be paid with both styles to cleaning the underlines of the branches. This imparts a marvellous floating feeling.

The Windswept style in principle should have the branches on the outer angle kept short or even removed while those on the inner angle are allowed to elongate. Branch placement on the inner angle may completely clothe the trunk from the base upwards or appear as a long thin pennant from the upper half or third. Branches should be given character by wiring and pruning to enhance the impression of force. The trunk in either style may be bent of straight according to taste. The stress is very much on branch shape. Roots should be raised quite sharply to anchor the trunk, and straight lines will reinforce the thrust of the tree.

CASCADE AND SEMI-CASCADE
Natural trees, nursery stock and any propagated material is suitable. Select low flattish trees with well developed lower

Leaning style: Long branches on outer angle

Windswept style: Tall variant

limbs in the case of the former two. Any of the other material may be shaped by wiring. Old sandpits and quarries are great places to hunt for natural material, as are mountainous areas.

Once established, this time in deep containers, propagation stock should be wire coiled and curved, first horizontally out over the pot rim then downwards in a series of steps connected by attractive curves that extend below the base of the pot. Cascade Bonsai therefore must be displayed on tall stands.

Traditionally the first step should swing in to break the line of the pot before snaking away again. The very formal cascade calls for a line of periphery that is almost vertical, or very steep in angle, with a head of foliage over the root lining up with the outermost tip. Other variations are less extreme and often feature a secondary or even multiple cascading trunks. The technique is always to create mounded-up pads of foliage resting on steps trained along outer bends. The pads should be of differing size and should relate to the bulk of the pot. They are made in the usual way in the herringbone style with wire and scissors but do try to create a domed cross-section in every case. An arrangement consisting of one major foliage dome and one medium, complemented by three smaller pads, would yield a good result.

Collected or nursery stock, being selected for potential, needs only wire coiling to enhance and bring out the style. Often a full cascade may be developed by wire coiling the

Cascade style: Classic variant

Cascade style: Informal variant

lowest limb of a large tree. The major trunk then being completely removed or severely shortened and trained to a complementary form. Such scars may be treated in the decorative jin style. See Chapter 8 on Pruning and Scar areas.

The Semi-Cascade style, again established in deep containers, follows a less extreme form and usually has one or more strong lower limbs that curve over the pot rim and up again in a gentle arc. These branches sometimes extend two or three feet and are balanced by an apex trained to dominate the pot area. Collected or nursery stock with heavy lower branch structure are the best material sources as to be successful the style should show a stout lower trunk beneath the first apex. Such material of course may be developed from propagation stock, but takes time. The method would be as for the Low Besom but with excess branching removed.

Semi-cascade style

CLASPED TO STONE; ROOT OVER STONE

Propagation stock or young trees are the best for the root over stone variant. The tree or trees should be pre-shaped so that no major manipulations disturb the root pattern. They should have long roots. Mate the shape of the tree to the rock, because as the tree develops it must always make a harmonious unit. A good selection would be a saddle stone having a taller buttress with the tree seated astride the stone like a jockey. The tree should project outwards from the rock with the head perhaps in alignment with the buttress. A low raking branch would successfully suggest space.

Having found a potential combination, shake some soil off the roots and try the tree on the stone at various angles. If there are vertical fissures in the stone, so much the better, as these will provide natural-looking channels to conduct the roots to the soil. Try not to disguise too much of the stone. When happy with the angle (sketch it if you are unsure of your memory), take the tree off the stone and wash all the soil off the roots. Take a mixture of peat/loam kneaded to a sloppy paste with water and apply it generously to the fissures chosen to channel the roots. Do not put any under the trunk base position. Replace the tree, check the angle and arrange the roots into bunches. Press them downwards into the paste areas all the way to the rock base so their tips may tuck underneath. Tie the tree in position by binding the stone in several directions with string or raffia. Do not use plastic or wire. The binding *must* rot. Do not use excessive pressure as the roots are easily damaged. Add more paste and press around the roots to ensure cover while they establish. Moss may be added to conserve moisture.

Lift the unit carefully and plant in a large temporary container with all root tips tucked carefully under the rock. Water carefully and place in the shade. Aftercare is as for other Bonsai but be extra careful with subsequent waterings as the soil tends to stay wet a long time near the stone. Light mistings are the best to maintain overall moisture.

Be very careful of the planting in the first year, but in the second the tree should be less delicate. Reserve any potential

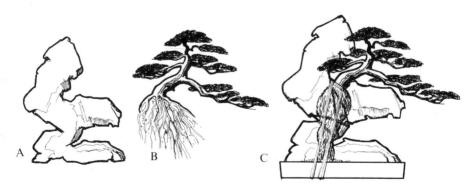

Clasped to stone style: Medium stone variant
A & B Stone and tree matched
C   Unit completed and tied down. Temporary container

root waggling operations for this time. Transfer to the final pot can take place in the third year. Accent plants such as small Azaleas or Ferns at the base of the stone will enhance the planting.

CLASPED TO STONE; ROOT CONFINED TO STONE
In this variant collected or nursery stock with good structures are the best. The tree should have a more or less finished shape. Low spreading trees look well with burly rocks with tough strata. When well done this variant can give the impression of an island or rocky cape. Bearing this in mind, try for as dramatic an arrangement as possible. When the position is fixed, wash some but not all soil from the root and try spreading the system in the chosen zone. Ideally this should be in a depression. If all looks well remove the tree. Make longish loops of covered wire and either glue them to the stone with quick-dry Epoxy, or, wrap one end in lead sheet and hammer this into convenient niches in the stone. Tie plastic-covered wires to the loops, long enough to meet comfortably over the roots. Spread a layer of Bonsai soil in the planting zone deep enough to accept half the root system and then replace the tree. Check angle. Settle the tree into the soil and tie the wires gently over the main root directions. Add more soil, probing and pushing it into the root system with the *fingers*. Never use sticks. When there are no more pockets ensure main root lines are clearly visible. If necessary remove a little soil around these to emphasize the line. Water the unit with a fine syringe or rose till saturated. Place a thin layer of peat/loam paste on the soil, leaving large roots exposed, and press *fine* textured moss on to the paste. The moss should be damp. Syringe again and aftercare is as before, but even more care should be taken to prevent drying in this style. If the planting stands on hidden blocks *just* clear of the surface in a tray of water, the humidity is increased and helps the foliage moisture greatly. Such trays are called Suibans and greatly add to the display value. Watering should always be gentle to prevent soil erosion. Feeding is vital with such restricted soil and should take place weekly. If the rock used is very hard, when repotting becomes necessary untie the wires and gently lift the tree so old roots may be cut and fresh soil given. Hard rocks offer less opportunity for the roots

to bind so this is usually successful. However if with softer rocks the roots have penetrated the surface and bonded to it there is more of a problem. Never attempt separation with such stones. If the tree looks off-colour consider converting it to the root over stone variant by allowing roots to travel down to a dish of soil prepared in the usual way. Another alternative is to sit the unit in a tray of soil prepared in the standard way and allow roots which appear through crevices to penetrate the soil. The tree will flourish again and if the soil is covered with decorative sand, the unit will still appear to be purely clasped to stone.

Clasped to stone style: Tall stone variant. Use of small trees increases perspective

Clasped to stone style: Flat stone variant

GROUPS

Fine featured plants are best which may be from collected, nursery stock or propagation material. The disposition has already been fully discussed so I will deal with the method. You will need trees with a compact and flat root system.

Select an oval or rectangular container of 45cm/18in or more in length, about 30cm/12in or more in width and the depth should not be less than 4cm/1½in. Pass as many strings (rotting variety) through the crocked drainage holes as you think are necessary to support the number of trees to be grouped. Prepare the container in the standard way half full with soil.

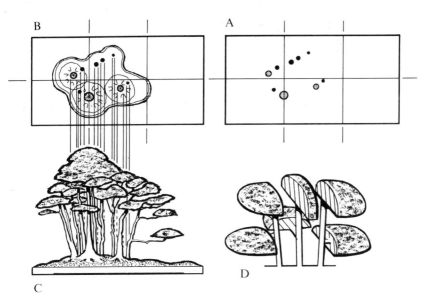

C

Group style: Nine tree variant
A Trunk placement
B Showing major foliage canopies
C Perspective view
D Sectional diagram illustrating group
   foliage pad placement after pruning

Arrange the trees according to disposition and elevate the main trees slightly by mounding the soil. Lead fishing weights or similar will be found handy to anchor roots while considering the effect. Temporary trunk ties also help. When satisfied with the arrangement, add further soil and fill any pockets with *finger* probing till the trees feel firmish. Remove location aids and tie the strings back and forth to steady the root systems. With additional soil, work carefully round the root masses contouring the soil and featuring surface roots. Peat/loam paste and moss may be added after watering. Water soil first. Remember, water weight on foliage causes trees to fall over, so saturate the soil before misting the trees. The aftercare is standard.

TWIN, TRIPLE, FIVE, SEVEN TRUNKS AND CLUMP
These styles have already largely been defined. In all cases the raising method is one where a balance of caliper is maintained in the trunks through a ratio of foliage weight.

Every trunk thickens according to the work it has to do in supporting foliage mass, therefore simply pruning to thin the foliage quota of minor trunks, balanced by boosted leaf production on major ones, will keep a varied appearance of thickness. Every three years the dominant trunks should be pruned hard all season to redress the balance. The minor ones, being allowed a season of free growth, soon pick up vigour. If they are still weak at the end of the season suppress the main trunks for another year and feed well.

Foliage tiers are treated according to taste. The secret of harmony is always to consider the whole unit when arranging the foliage. Deciduous trees normally have rounded foliage pads whilst those of conifers are normally flattish or down-swept. Whichever you decide on preserve the line throughout, but make variations in step heights and size of the pads. Always keep trunk lines clear of young shoot and foliage peripheries neat and well defined. An overall rounded parasol form or a rough triangle are usually pleasing. Preserve harmony in trunks and try to make them echo the shapes of the key trees. Material for the multiple trunk styles are easily found growing wild. There are superb examples of Scots Pine to be found.

Root connected style:
Seven tree variant

Group style: Cluster variant

RAFT STYLE

It is normally better to begin with a young tree from propagation stock when forming the raft. Trunks of 30-45cm/12-18in are convenient in size.

A large temporary container is prepared, big enough to accept the whole tree when laid flat. Trees may be prepared for raft treatment one year or more in advance if desired.

The branches are wired to one side of the trunk. Any growing diametrically opposite the wired side should be removed, as the idea is to lay the tree down on the denuded side. Any side branches may be retained and spread sideways in the herringbone. A form like a tennis raquet should evolve. The newly arranged branches should have their tips elevated as these will become 'trees'. Those branches in the centre, growing straight up from the trunk, will form the spine of the raft and in the pre-shaping season the lower branches should be encouraged to grow thick by pruning the upper portions of the tree heavily.

In the following year any wires should be removed. Remove sections of bark on the naked side of the trunk. These should be about $2\frac{1}{2}$cm/1in long and no more than one third of the diameter in width. Dust the wounds with hormone rooting powder. Make the wounds near old branch points. This encourages rooting.

Lay the tree flat in the container on a bed of soil either straight along the container or diagonally. A diagonal arrangement gives greater perspective. Further soil may be added to cover or half cover the trunk as desired. Heap soil over the root nucleus. Water in well and use standard aftercare, but leave the container strictly undisturbed.

The new 'trees' may be gently pruned as they develop to encourage style according to height desired. Take care not to disturb the buried trunk.

In the third season the raft should be gently taken out of the container and some soil should be washed off to see how rooting is progressing. If new roots from the trunk and main branches are equal in volume to the old root, all is well. Cut the old system off completely and establish the raft in the container for another year. Be very careful with the new roots—they are as delicate as those of new cuttings. If new roots are

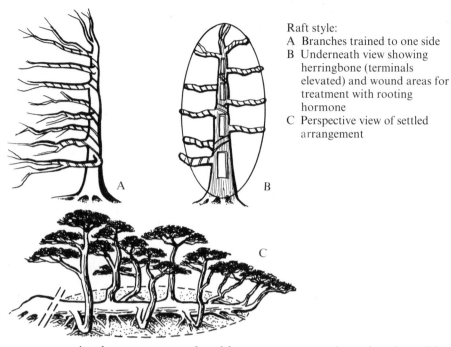

Raft style:
A Branches trained to one side
B Underneath view showing herringbone (terminals elevated) and wound areas for treatment with rooting hormone
C Perspective view of settled arrangement

inadequate, prune the old root mass severely and replant. The extra year will normally do the trick.

ROOT CONNECTED

It is worth searching for natural examples in hedgerows. Failing this, propagation stock of suitable suckering species will quickly yield results. Prepare a container large enough to take the whole system without cramping and surface as many major roots as possible. Establish and feed well. Next season reduce the height of the tree by two thirds or more. Elms will quickly produce suckers from strong roots as a result. If the dominant parent trunk is suppressed while the new shoots are establishing, this style may be created very quickly. Wire shaping may be carried out in the second season of 'forest' growth. The rules of perspective for this style and the raft are as for the group. The forms themselves are again limitless and bounded only by species suitability. An Elm for example would make a superb Besom forest in either style. The spine of the trunk in the raft should be emphasized and in either style, the

28

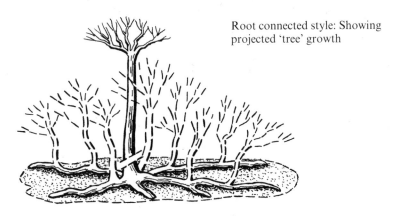

Root connected style: Showing projected 'tree' growth

linked-limb ground pattern should be clearly defined. As the planting matures, surface roots will thicken and add further interest.

The Bonsai Process

This will be described in detail after the chapters on Seedling etc, which feature every main process in action. Bonsai is a culmination of many techniques.

3   RAISING BONSAI FROM SEEDLINGS

YEAR ONE

The simplest method of raising a dwarf tree is to begin by planting a seed in a pot. The choice of seed is wide and only limited by desirable, neat appearance characteristics of the parent plant. Scale is important in Bonsai and so a choice of fine featured plant like Cotoneaster for instance will yield a better result than a Sycamore.

A little study of the best season for seed collecting of various species will go a long way to guarantee success. Information is readily available so I have not included it in this book.

SEED COMPOST

The seed should be sown in an appropriate soil mix such as John Innes seed compost. Ensure the pot has ample drainage holes and place a crocking disc over these followed by a good layer of really open gravel as a drainage course. A good layer of compost follows and if heavy or overfine, dry it in an oven then sieve it to remove the fine particles and overlarge clods. An ideal seed compost should be open in texture with no particle finer than 1.5mm/$\frac{1}{16}$in. Tap the pot wall to settle the compost and gently level it to 2$\frac{1}{2}$cm/1in from the rim, pop the seed in and press it till half covered then gently scatter further compost over, level again and water in well. This method applies whatever your choice of pot: a flower pot; a seed tray; a drilled-out yoghurt container or pâté jar—all will work satisfactorily if you follow the standard method.

Place the pot in a shady place and withhold water till the soil looks and feels dryish and then water again. A dampish soil is the ideal—sogginess invites rot.

Placement should be in a frost-free area with good ventilation and light. Shade is only an initial requirement.

When seeds germinate and break the soil, water/spray them with a systemic fungicide. This, if repeated as the seedlings develop, almost makes rot or damp-off a thing of the past—do not neglect it and repeat it every two weeks.

Gradually over some days allow the seedlings more light till full light is reached. After a period true leaves appear. The first set are cotyledons and should be disregarded. The growing apex elongates steadily and side leaves appear which begin to show typical characteristics. A pine seedling is somewhat of an exception in that leaves are often bunched and juvenile in the first season but come true in the second.

A few weeks after the second set of leaves appear, feed the seedlings with a dilute feed solution. Any of the excellent proprietary brands will do. This provides a quick release of food and ensures even development. Repeat every two weeks. Continue the water/feed/fungicide regime until dormancy. Feeding stops completely by September. Seedlings are normally woody or going firm by this time and the fungicide also stops.

Watering is governed by observation. During the earlier active growing season water is needed often, but during winter, when temperatures are lower, the soil stays moist far longer. Whatever the period, if the soil when scratched appears darker underneath there is enough water present. Check regularly.

Placement over winter remains the same: frost-free with good light and ventilation.

No shaping of the tree has been attempted because the rule is always sound establishment first. The open soil used and the water and feed regime followed will have developed a strong plant. The soil enables water and air to pass through rapidly, enabling sound roots to develop. Feeding causes the roots to multiply to take it up and the root development directly effects the top growth which will be strong with dominant resting buds ready for year 2.

YEAR 2

Assuming the seedlings are sturdy little plants 8-10cm/3-4in high, transplant them when their buds begin to swell. If they are smaller than this, or a little spindly, leave them and repeat the schedule of year 1.

TRANSPLANTING

Tap the seedlings out of the pot or container and using a high pressure water jet wash off the soil. Gently tease apart the tangle of roots. If of course you have planted singly the problem is easier.

Provided there is a good growth of roots, remove any long roots and tip back any heavier roots by one third. Even out the root mass. Use *sharp, clean* scissors. If the root is meagre, gently unravel it but do not cut.

Select a new pot which is big enough to house the horizontally spread root mass without cramping and provide at least 8cm/3in of soil depth. Prepare container as before but a little extra sieved leaf mould may be added—coarse particles only—say $\frac{1}{2}$ part by bulk. All soil mixed dry as before.

With the soil levelled off to below $2\frac{1}{2}$cm/1in of the pot rim, take the seedling and spread the roots radially. Be gentle! Sit it in the soil. Take time over the root arragement and try for as uniform an arrangement as possible. Think of the spokes of a wheel with the stem as the hub. The seedling should seem and feel to 'sit' naturally. This process is a *must* for all Bonsai. The radial system encourages a buttress at the base of the trunk which leads to the flair line seen on all old trees. It also promotes a good even development in the top growth and so a mirror image emerges—as the root ramifies so does the top growth and vice versa. This reciprocal state is probably the least recognized yet one of the cardinal points of success in Bonsai of quality.

Add at least a $1\cdot25$cm/$\frac{1}{2}$in of soil over the spread root system to anchor the seedling securely, level off neatly and water in well. The shade to light and build-up to regular watering/feed schedules are as Year 1. Start feeding four weeks after transplanting. This will have given any root wounds time to seal; premature feeding will injure them. A light misting of water over the leaves daily during the shaded period helps establishment. It helps to maintain the moisture content of the plant till the roots can take up the regular requirement again.

Seedling: Initial root pruning

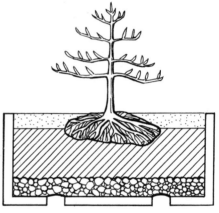

Seedling: Roots spread radially after initial pruning

By mid-summer of this second season shaping may begin. In this first instance the leading shoot is pinched back to one pair of leaves on year two growth. Pinch back more lightly in the case of a Pine. The immediate result, if they are not already moving, is a great burst of activity from the side shoots.

It is good practice to give an extra feed the week before the initial pinch to provide extra energy.

Remove alternate buds up the trunk. A typical bud selection for branch structure might be: left low, right higher, third bud higher to rear and repeat to apex. Remove all others.

Opposite Mountain Maple over stone (30 years)

This technique opens the framework for artistic reasons—it will be seen that old trees shed opposing branches, producing a marvellously characterful branch pattern. The technique also helps the health of the tree, as the negative areas created permit light and air to reach every portion of the plant, thus keeping it strong. The third function is that of energy channelling: only the chosen points will develop.

After 3-4 weeks the buds make strong side shoots and these should be left till they have formed 3-4 sets of leaves. In the case of the pine, shoots should be permitted 5-8cm/2-3in of extension—this will take longer but be patient.

As new apex growths appear, select one which blends in line with the top retained branch and remove all others. Let the new leading shoot develop 3-4 sets of leaves and then pinch back to two sets. Deal with other high branches in the same way.

The principle is the same as for hedge trimming: top suppression gives bushiness and strong growth from the base. In Bonsai, when pruning, whatever the age of the species involved, be severe at the top of the tree and phase out the degree like a cone to the base. This keeps a good vigour balance in the tree. Remember to increase feeding.

Maintain the cone schedule of shoot removal during the season and wonder of wonders, joy of joys—your seedling begins to look like a little tree as autumn approaches.

A deciduous or fast-growing species will be more advanced than a Pine, but that is a matter of growth rate. If the

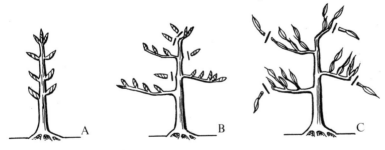

Seedling: A Typical bud habit
 B Removal of opposite buds
 C Tipping terminals

Opposite Japanese Cedar (40 years)

35

techniques are followed (see the section on Bonsai Data) for a few seasons the pine will soon look bushy and satisfying, so do not be discouraged.

As year 2 closes, make plans for shape potential. Study natural tree forms during the winter and get a feel for natural branch development. Notice the subtle differences between Oak, Chestnut, Beech, and Elm. All are basically the upturned broom shape called Besom in Bonsai terminology. Imagine the form scaled down and applied to the seedlings.

YEAR 3

The chosen seedlings are fed weekly from bud-swelling onwards for strength. Around the end of April the seedlings are ready for shaping (delay Pines till August) this is carried out with wire coiling and deep pruning.

Plastic covered wire is safest for young Bonsai—there is no risk of metal contamination and the plastic reduces friction.

As you will see from the recommended styles, there is considerable flexibility in form suitable for each species.

As the informal style is the most popular I will choose it for demonstration. The informal style features a gently curved trunk generally in a lazy S-shape: if the primary base curve swings to the left, the secondary will flow to the right. The major branches are trained to project outwards and downwards from the outer angle of curve. By referring to the selected branch pattern of Year 2, a mental picture evolves of the curving necessary to establish the style. Usually beginners make the mistake of curving the trunk snake-fashion, two-dimensionally. To avoid this, take the tree backwards from the trunk base and forwards from about the midway point. A three-dimensional feeling results which adds immediately to charm. Try to arrange matters so the third branch can be glimpsed through the framework.

Have several different grades of wire handy. Gently, using thumbs and forefingers of both hands, flex the seedling. Feel and note the trunk strength. Flex test the wire in the same way: equal resistance means the gauge is about right.

Remove any soil debris and feel for major root locations with the fingers and mark their location. The piece of wire will have to be about 3-4 inches longer than the height of the plant.

Insert the wire into the soil, close to the trunk, and avoid the main roots! Thrust firmly into the soil to prevent shifting. Using this an an anchor, begin very gently to coil the wire in an upward spiral round the trunk. Coil evenly and make sure the wire is just in contact with the bark. On a 15-20cm/6-8in seedling, coils about 1.25cm/$\frac{1}{2}$in apart will be right. Do not pin any branches or foliage on the way and try to arrange coiling so the wire is on the outside of an intended bend. This gives positive tension at the angle. Finish wiring to the top but avoid damage to the apex.

That is the principle and the best thing to do is to chop a lump off the nearest shrub of equivalent thickness and coil and recoil that till you are happy about the feel of wiring. It's only a knack! When practising, try taking the strain of the wire in the fingers rather than grinding into the trunk.

Taking it very gently, place the thumbs under the point to be curved, fingers on top, and slowly bend the trunk. Watch the trunk and listen intently. If horizontal cracks are seen opening on the bend or if ominous creaks are heard, it is bent enough at that point for one year! Move on to the second bend and third and so on.

Larger more dynamic curves are best at the base and lesser ones further up. Wiring is the most difficult process for most people, so if the first effort is ungainly carry on with number two. The main thing is the ice is broken and even the second attempt is easier.

Slight readjustments and finer bends are in order, but do not make major re-bends. Wiring creates changes in the cell structure: on the outer bend cells are ruptured and compressed on the inner angle. If, therefore, the limb once bent is immediately re-bent in a different direction, the chances are most cells will be ruptured and extensive die-back if not death itself results.

After wiring, the cells readjust to the new line and after a period settle into the imposed shape. The area is then 'set' and is dewired.

Flex test the branches and match the wire. Ideal anchorage points for the wire are the bases of opposing branches. Coil the wire from the anchorage round the trunk and along the limb. Bend the branches to the design.

Wire shaping: Main trunk

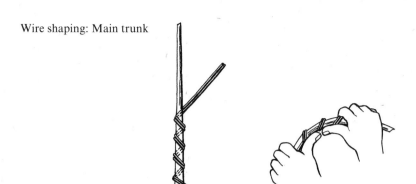

Coiling trunk   First bend

Old trees in the main have weeping branches and as one of the objects of Bonsai is to convey age, a gentle downward sweep will convey this but elevate each branch terminal slightly. Branches lose vigour if the terminal is not allowed a vertical type of placement. Equally, if a lower branch loses vigour at some future date, vigour is normally quickly regained by raising vertically.

Now assess the tree and check that the design is fully three-dimensional. This much-overlooked detail gives great quality. The branches should be seen clearly separated with no conflict of line and the back branches complete the form.

Arrange any side shoots so the underlines of the main branches remain clean. The time has now come to add further character by pruning. If a bud is chosen near a curved twig section that points in an abruptly different direction, pruning ahead of the bud will cause it to shoot and thus give a kink in the branch. This may be repeated on the ensuing shoot. A mixture of this fine pruning and wire curving along branch planes will give a satisfyingly diverse structure. Finally, arrange the branch periphery as neatly as possible.

After 'the treatment', shade the trees for a few days. Give it a holiday with plenty of feed to strengthen it after the ordeal. Carefully check to see no wires are 'biting' into the structure anywhere and do this weekly—young trees grow fast.

With all the seedlings, periodically reinforce the vigour cones by pruning the tree lightly in the way suggested. Clean out any

Second bend

Main curves complete.
Front view

Side view. Front facing
left. Note trunk form

crossing growths or basal shoots at trunk/branch junctions
that threaten trained branches. These often grow at a terrific
rate and will inhibit the development of desirable limbs. Old
trees it will be noted have no such 'in-growths'.

Feed all trees on a weekly basis till September but gradually
diminish the amount.

Wire shaping: Major branches
A Branches cleaned
B Branches arranged in
   contra-relation to trunk
C Typical foliage pad

YEAR 4

Most people pot their seedlings at this stage and if small trees are the aim, it is arguable that this is the best course. However, for trunk fattening a period of free growth is desirable.

Either prepare an area in the garden by digging it over and working in plenty of leaf mould, peat and a few handfuls of bonemeal, leave it in fine tilth and plant the trees in this; or, prepare large temporary containers such as wooden seed-trays and fill with a mixture of one part John Innes No 2, one part sifted leaf mould and three parts coarse sand and plant trees one to a container only. Ground planted trees should be spaced so there is at least a clear 23cm/9in between neighbouring branch tips.

Open ground gives faster thickening, but the container, whilst slower, gives mobility for training.

In either case, spread the root system with the fingers in as radial a fashion as possible. Trim away any dominant roots and lightly even the root mass, as at transplanting time in Year 2. Water in well.

After about four weeks of growth in ground or box, begin feeding on a weekly basis till September. A foliar feed is a useful auxiliary at this time.

Allow the shoots to rampage a little, say to 4-5 pairs of leaves before shortening back. Be careful not to overdo the growth as too much space between leaf pairs, called nodes, is ugly. Short internodal length in Bonsai is important. A little trial and error will soon give the idea.

Keep established lines distinct by pinching and pruning, but allow the trunk and branches to evolve if you want a bigger Bonsai. Aim for an upturned saucer appearance over each branch plane.

By mid-season, a gratifyingly dense twig growth is noticeable and trunk expansion will be starting.

Grooming will probably be necessary on a monthly basis once the tree is firmly rooted. Do not attempt any wiring in this season. The trees will be better for it.

Spray routinely for protection against insects. Once a fortnight use pyrethrum, but should bugs become immune vary the spraying with 'systemic' insecticide. Dilute the spray to slightly less than recommended rates.

By the autumn, increases in trunk caliper will be measurable. Trees in boxes may be given light frost protection but those in open ground should be able to stand low temperatures.

YEAR 5

If the trunk has now reached sufficient caliper, those in open growth may be lifted at repotting time and potted in suitable containers. If further development is required, leave them undisturbed and continue top maintenance. Those in boxes if now acceptable in thickness should also be potted. However, I would personally advocate reversing the roles of those in boxes and those in ground for a season. If as much as two seasons are allowed between role reversals a remarkable development takes place.

If the tree is to be potted, a container with certain characteristics is vital. These are: adequate drainage holes; porous or semi-porous body; suitable root run space; appropriate texture and colour.

Prepare the pot by first soaking for a day in water. This will help neutralize any minerals that may be present—harmless to the tree—annoying visually, which declare themselves as white deposits. If these do appear, a scouring pad and water will remove them and a light oiling with vegetable oil will also dispel them.

Dry the pot and prepare plastic netting crocking discs. The plastic netting can be obtained at most garden centres. Prepare a U-shaped piece of wire for each drainage hole. The width of the U should match the width of the drainage hole. Locate the netting over the holes and pass the prongs of each U downwards through holes till the base of each U is in contact with the netting. If the U legs are then bent out sideways flat against the underside of the pot, the mesh cannot move. If a very small pot is used, just cut a piece of net large enough to lay flat wall-to-wall on the inside floor of the pot and forget the locating wires.

Pass strings or covered wires up through the holes (threaded underneath from hole to hole) which are long enough to meet generously in the pot centre.

Add a covering of coarse sand as a drainage course. This will vary with the depth of the pot eg, if a pot with 5cm/2in inner depth is used then 6mm/$\frac{1}{4}$in of sand is adequate. Take a good layer of main soil, bone-dry and well sifted (to remove any particle less than 3mm/$\frac{1}{8}$in size) and spread enough for the root mass to sit on showing the trunk base flush, or a little raised above the pot rim.

Site the tree so that from the front it is seen a little to the rear of pot centre and to one side or another of the long axis centre point. An idea placement is with the trunk centre at $\frac{1}{3}$ of the way along the major axis.

The decision as to which end to plant is dictated by the weight of branch development and trunk inclination. If heavy to left then plant $\frac{1}{3}$ right with the mass overhanging the $\frac{2}{3}$, or vice versa. This is a cardinal rule in assymetry, where balance is achieved by counterpoise, rather than in even balance as usually accepted in the west.

Tie the strings over the root mass so the tree cannot shift. Do not use force, a light restraint is all that is necessary. Water the tree well with a gentle spray. Water the soil first and then the mass of the tree. If this is not done in this sequence, the whole tree will topple with the weight of water. Aftercare is exactly as before, as are subsequent repottings.

4 CUTTINGS

Cuttings are much quicker than seedlings and have the advantage of adult characteristics, eg, there will be no wait for blooms on flowering subjects as with a seedling. It is a reliable means to increase plant material for Bonsai with desirable characteristics, such as bark or neat foliage habit, whereas seed will usually only come true on a random basis.

Plants I have personally found to be reliable as Bonsai subjects from cuttings include: TRIDENT MAPLE, CHINESE ELM, MOUNTAIN MAPLE, WILLOW, HORNBEAM, COTONEASTER, AZALEA, JASMINE, FIRETHORN, QUINCE, ZELKOVA, JUNIPER, CYPRESS, YEW and CRYPTOMERIA.

With the exception of Yew, which is taken from January to March from previous season's wood, all the others are taken from current year wood which has just gone firm at the base.

The soft tip is removed and all foliage is stripped for a 5cm/2in zone up from the stem base. This should leave 2-3 sets of leaves intact at the top of the cutting. Recut the cutting base with sharp, sterile scissors; dip base in rooting hormone powder (match strength to species) and insert in an open, well-ventilated and draining rooting medium, in a seed box or similar. Water in well—if cuttings are long, soak from the base so as to prevent disturbance. Close box with clear polythene to retain moisture. Remove cover and *mist* foliage twice daily. After 2-3 days spray with systemic fungicide. If taken in May/June period most subjects root without difficulty in 3-4 weeks. Allow a good system of roots to develop and then gently transplant cuttings into containers, using standard soil mix. Handle roots as little as possible as initially they are incredibly brittle.

After 3-4 weeks in shade with careful watering, give a dilute feed weekly through till September. Maintain foliage moisture throughout. Cuttings have at least a two year start on seedlings and as you experiment you will find there are some species—willow for example—that will root from quite old wood. This gives a tremendous start as pre-shaped material can be used. two year old wood of other subjects may routinely be wire-shaped before treatment as cuttings. After a year of establishment care is as for seedlings, but with the inbuilt advantages of plant maturity.

 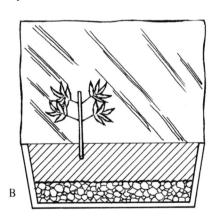

Cuttings:
A Cutting prepared   B Cutting inserted

5 LAYERING AND GRAFTING

Layerings are a step further on from cuttings in the scope they offer for selection of pre-shaped material for Bonsai. It is possible and desirable to work on branch areas chosen for layerings because this is the method whereby picturesque Bonsai of any form may be rooted and detached from the donor tree. In Japan, donor trees are frequently planted for this purpose. *Picea glehnii,* the SAGHALIN SPRUCE, is a notable example.

Spring
Assuming you find a section of branch tip that is pleasingly shaped, or upon which you have worked, the standard method is followed.

Make cuts down to the heartwood with a razor blade, girdling the limb apart from the bridge of entire bark 3mm/⅛in wide, which must be left intact. If a multiple trunk Bonsai is envisaged, make the top cut close under the existing forking. If a single trunk is the object, assess the amount of space desired

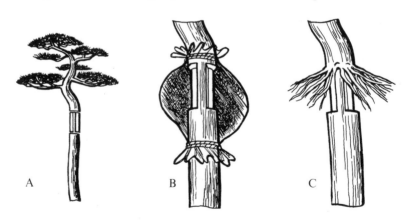

Layering:
A Branch tip preshaped ready for layering
B Area stripped of bark except 3mm/⅛in bridge. Hormone treated and wrapped with moist peat inside plastic
C Area 2-3 months later. In fact moss would be left intact. Plant is then detached below new roots

between root and first branch, Then make the top cut at that point. Make the second cut about 2·5cm-5cm/1-2in remote from the first, preserve the 3mm/⅛in bridge intact, then peel off the bark, exposing the bare heartwood. Dust this with rooting hormone powder. Take two handfuls of sphagnum moss and saturate it in water, then wring it out. Secure a sheet of polythene film around and below the second cut, pack the wound area with wet moss, draw up the film around the moss and secure well above the top cut. Make sure of close contact over the moss to inhibit evaporation. Open the top monthly to check for moss dampness and reseal.

Given average luck on your first attempt, roots will appear and the layering will be detachable within the year, if done early enough. March/April is ideal.

Aftercare is similar to that of cuttings. Be careful with the mossed area, perhaps just leaving it intact. Establish well and the result is a Bonsai ready for potting inside two years.

GRAFTING

One of the few Bonsai commonly grafted in Japan is the 5-needle Pine. This is done to reproduce the precise characteristics of the donor tree, in commercially viable numbers. The tree also grows faster, according to some authorities, in a grafted form. I have included a standard method.

Potted stocks of Black, Red or Scots Pine may be used. They should be well-established two year olds. They may be brought into a greenhouse or warm place in October and kept there till January/February, when grafting takes place. The trick is to ensure dormancy of the scion and growth activity in the stock. Take strongly grown 5-8cm/2-3in twigs of previous season wood of 5-needle Pine, removing the basal 2·5cm/1in of the needle growth that will be clothing the twig. With a clean, razor-edged knife, make a downward, diagonal slit in the trunk of the stock. Penetrate about ⅓ of the trunk diameter. Angle of slit should be about 30°-45° and the cut should be about 1·25-2cm/½-¾in long. Measure the upper and lower faces of the expanded slit (opened enough to accommodate the scion) then wedge-cut de-needled 5-needle Pine scion to match. Bend the stock to open the slit and insert the scion wedge to mate up. Ensure the outer bark aligns exactly on at least one side of the slit. Paint the wound area heavily with tree seal paint so no air can penetrate, wrap the union with polythene film to locate it and tie firmly. Water well and cover over the graft. Some people place the graft inside a greenhouse, with bottom heat; others simply place a jam jar over the whole unit. The great thing is to maintain moisture throughout the system of the graft. The Japanese even go as far as earthing up the union. Whatever the finer points, keep the graft moist; after about three months there should be definite bud activity on the scion, if the graft has taken. After this has become apparent, feed the graft regularly till September. Remove the remaining section of stock trunk above the graft after one year. Most people agree grafting should take place at the trunk base where the future earth line can disguise the union.

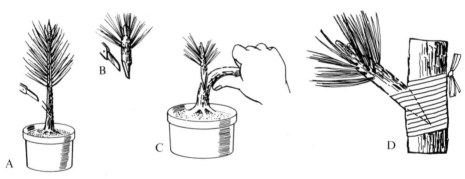

Grafting:
A Black Pine stock with cleft incision
B White Pine scion trimmed to fine wedge
C Stock bent to admit scion
D Union bound to prevent shifting

6 NURSERY STOCK

This, either potted or in open growth, offers a good opportunity to gain an instant trunk. Look for trunk taper and a compact, low-growing branch system. Reference to the sections on Styles will be useful in selecting material.

Possible species to look for would be Japanese Maples and Junipers, both often potted. The Maples by their nature assume picturesque shapes, so try in addition to find specimens with good roots (flared evenly) with at least two to three strong lower branches.

Junipers (those with tree forms) quickly thicken and become more difficult to shape, so if a heavy trunked tree is found, be sure it already has a characterful form. If straight, consider training it in the upright style. Shrubby Junipers often form multi or cascading trunks and can quickly be converted into Bonsai of charm.

Azaleas and Cotoneasters are also good subjects to look for and are often found potted. Look for Azaleas with single, or at most, triple trunks.

Cotoneasters are again usually found with multiple trunks due in part to pinching and to their natural habit, but careful searching usually unearths at least one single trunked speci-men. The trunk, as with Azaleas, is brittle so pre-formed trunk shape is of importance. If a change of direction is required, it is best achieved by deep pruning. Both these subjects react very well to such pruning.

Try to select material which has a good colour and seems free of discoloured areas generally. Avoid anything that has a lot of die-back. This usually indicates root strangulation, or at best the material will not have been growing actively for some time.

When you reach home the first thing to do is put the trees at a convenient height, and assess each one.

Assuming the trees are the usual garden centre products, the typical solution will be conversion to Informal Upright style. The fun with nursery stock comes in arranging foliage masses into pleasing lines around the main axis line of the trunk. Again, the rules of assymetry apply. Relating every cut to the preconceived plan, remove all minor growths masking main lines. This clarifies the structure and makes work much easier.

If you regard each branch plane as an ellipse, offset horizontally from the trunk, this also helps the decision to retain or sacrifice.

Try to arrange matters so the first lower branch goes left or right; the second, higher, to the opposing side, and the third, to the back.

Clean out twigs close into the trunk and those that plunge below the horizontal or each main branch. Strong vertical twigs should be eliminated or pruned back severely so that future growths 'break' horizontally.

As you prune towards the head or apex of the tree, assess branch length and placement. Usually the extreme head, or apical cluster of a Bonsai is, or should be, small and simple. Careful scrutiny of old Bonsai or natural trees reveals that in fact the broad, domed head is in reality the effect of many, not any one, single branch ends.

It is important to bear this fact in mind. If the head is kept small (however exquisitely shaped) and a triangle/cone of branch length is encouraged, you have achieved the cone vigour index mentioned earlier.

Place the tree on the ground. From overhead, the branches should appear spoke-like from the limb of the trunk. Arrange every branch by wire coiling so, from above, no limb overlaps.

Replace tree at viewing height and make the wire coiling adjustments necessary to achieve radial positions. If wiring threatens to break limbs, a little aerial cross-tying will often solve the problem. Cushion pressure/friction areas with soft rag, rubber tubing or similar. Do not wrap the tree with adhesive tape as this often wrecks the bark later. Consider the trunk: with branches in major positions, the most challenging and exciting stage of training has arrived! The trunk awaits the magic touch!

If the material is already naturally shaped, the work is easy and consists of simply arranging the tiered branch ellipses into outward, gently down-curving masses from the main trunk curves. If the species dictates (eg Apricot, Senkaki Maple), wrap the wire in masking tape to protect the bark before use.

In all wiring, the space between coils is the determining control factor. If therefore you have an exaggerated base curve balanced with finer bends higher up, make sure the coils are placed accordingly.

Think carefully before bending! Remember re-bending can damage tissue. Bear in mind also the three-dimensional aspect of the trunk. The most interesting Bonsai are those with depth.

In general terms too, it is good not to wire tightly, particularly for the novice. It is kinder to the tree, if necessary, to have another go in two years' time at the final shape, than to cripple the tree at the outset with too much wire.

If splitting occurs in wiring try not to panic—merely leave that zone without further bending and attend to the next area. When you have finished the trunk apply tree wound paint to any damaged areas. The tree is not going to die in ten minutes and finishing the job saves getting bitumen up the elbows.

Work carefully through each area of the trunk making minor bend adjustments and then through each branch. Adjust twigs with wire later when the plant has had a rest of a month or two and some good feeds.

Your tree which is styled according to the time for the species, should be pampered for a year before potting in a container, if the trunk justifies it. If the trunk needs 'beef', remember the ground/box combination.

7   COLLECTING NATURAL TREES

First obtain permission to dig from the landowner.
1 In the Spring when new growth is just apparent, cut a 30-45cm/12-18in diameter circle round the trunk of the tree with a spade. Make the spade cut at least a spit deep and incline it outwards. Make a second cut 8cm/3in inside the first.
2 Remove the soil inside the trench created, to the depth of the cut. Replace with moistened leaf mould and sharp sand. Clean any ragged ends with secateurs. Fine roots will form from the cut root ends. These are ciliary or feeder roots and their presence determines the survival of the tree. The tree must be left in situ until these have formed, which is usually a year or two.
3 Prune the top of the tree as seems indicated. It is best to lighten the head of the tree somewhat as this always encourages lower branches. In Bonsai, the lower branches should be thicker to maintain visual balance and natural appearance, so prune more lightly towards the base. Trunks thicken according to the number of branches. Branches thicken according to the number of sub branches and twigs so in pruning remember this and try to aim for a balance of vigour.

4 In the following spring, if the fine roots have developed well, cut the remaining lower roots and remove the tree. Retain as much soil as possible. Wrap the root ball in moist sphagnum moss, tie with string and wrap tree in a polythene bag after spraying the foliage with water.

5 On reaching home, carefully unwrap the root ball and depending on root production in relation to the tree as a whole, either plant it in a large tub or box, or a regular Bonsai pot. The decision will depend on whether to pot a Bonsai means further root cutting. If it does—do not risk it! Plant in the box.

6 In either case ample drainage holes are vital. Place crocking over holes. At least 2·5cm/1in coarse sand over crocking. Mix 1 part John Innes No 2, 1 part sifted leaf mould, 3 parts coarse sand. This should be mixed dry. Place layer of mix on sand course, rest tree on the soil and work soil around the roots and upwards to within 1·25cm/$\frac{1}{2}$in of lip of box or container.

Ensure the soil is in contact with all aspects of the root ball and all spaces are filled. Fingers are best to feel for pockets and to firm soil. Never press hard. If necessary tie tree in the pot.

7 Water whole tree and soil with fine spray till water trickles from the drainage holes. Water soil carefully and if it dries around trunk water again but normally wait a week. Never let the soil become soggy in the vital first six weeks.

8 Place tree in shade where no wind, rain or sun can reach it for two to four weeks. Feed tree after six weeks.

9 If tree is evergreen, water-spray plant twice a day, otherwise once a day. New buds should appear and grow after three to four weeks. Gradually introduce the tree to more light, but be cautious for the first year.

10 Let the tree establish solidly for at least two seasons then gradually reduce the size of the roots over one or more years till they will fit the Bonsai pot of your choice. Do not wire train the plant until at least twelve months after potting and only then if it is strong.

Opposite top Chinese Elm (40 years)
Opposite bottom Red Maple (30 years)

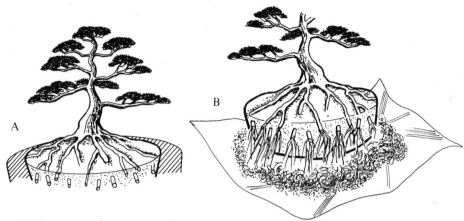

Collecting a natural tree:
A Tree with trench excavated and root ends cleaned. Trench is filled with leaf mould and sharp sand
B Tree one or two years later with line feeder roots developed. Tree has had lower roots cut and will be wrapped in moss and polythene

8   THE BONSAI PROCESS

PRUNING

Pruning is the process by which the foliage texture is controlled. Theoretically it should leave no scars as it is carried out during active growth periods on very soft extending tissue which heals quickly. In practice, as pruning also means removal of older wood, some scarring is inevitable. There are a number of ways in which this can be disguised and indeed utilized in the design.

Most deciduous trees are pruned by pinching back soft new shoots. From 2-5 pairs of leaves are allowed to develop. These will appear at regular intervals along the extending shoot. If pruning is done prior to this point of extension, very dwarf growth results which will then develop slowly. It is a point to remember when you have a finished tree. With the developing tree the longer shoots provide greater flexibility in design use.

Opposite top Trident Maple Raft–August 1977

Opposite bottom Trident Maple Raft–Winter 1978 (90 years)

They will react strongly when pinched back and stand a far better chance of survival if you choose to wire shape them. The degree to which the shoot is pinched back depends once again on the position and function of the donor twig. At the apex such shoots are pinched back to one pair of leaves. Lateral tips are likewise dealt with fairly firmly, bearing in mind the vigour cone. Never prune to the same degree over the whole tree. Pruning into older wood may be carried out for various reasons; one being angle changes in branching. This is a useful means of building an interesting structure.

Pruning above buds that point in the desired direction triggers the latent bud. This is allowed to grow till buds are clearly seen on the new shoot. Re-select the shape direction and prune again. Thus a natural-looking accumulation of kinks appears in the limb. If those are softened by wiring here and there, a real feeling of character evolves. Other reasons for old wood pruning are to stimulate internally placed latent buds or to prevent total overgrowth. As with a Maple, where periodically some branch length reduction has to be carried out to check extending lines. Trees which are well pruned using a combination of both methods, show pleasantly neat foliage as

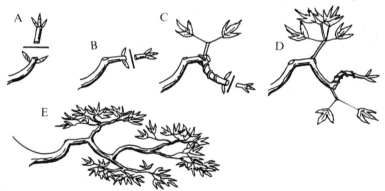

Pruning: Branch character
A Terminal removed, shoot breaks sideways
B Terminal removed, shoot breaks sideways; top is kept short, lower allowed full rein then wired
C Terminal removed, shoot breaks sideways
D Wired top extension shoot and lower shoot
E The vigorous shoots have become the main branch and minor shoots are now minor side branches

a result. The underlying structure is also interesting and will have short twigging. Heavy limb removal in shaping a tree at any stage should be considered not only in terms of the negative space created, but also whether the resultant scar may be used in the design. With evergreens, rather than total branch removal, consider leaving a snag which may be peeled of bark and thereby contribute an aged appearance to the area. Trees in nature, particularly Pines, display this phenomenon. If a snag, or jin as it is known in Japanese, will fit in with the shape of the tree and add something positive, then do it, but not for its own sake!

The method for jin is to break rather than cut the redundant limb at a suitably imposing length visually. A break will look better than a scissor cut. Ring the bark of the limb at the tree line, then cut laterally along the limb and peel off the bark. A live branch will shed bark easily but if the limb is already dead the bark can be tenacious, so use a sharp knife to shave it off. With a newly peeled jin shaped from fresh wood, a drying time of 2 to 3 months must elapse for the wood to dry naturally. When this is passed, paint the limb with neat lime/sulphur compound. Be careful, paint slowly with a fine brush and do not get any compound on yourself, live foliage or soil area. Place the tree in a sunny spot and the compound will gradually change from a revolting apple green to a pleasant bleached white over 2-3 days. This gives one a nicely aged trunk detail but also the compound preserves the dead wood from rotting. The compound should be applied twice a year in sunny weather for 2-3 years for permanent preservation. Wash the jin surface before re-applying with a toothbrush and clean water. A final point of interest in jin creation is that newly peeled wood can in fact be wired into a pleasing shape and when dried out, the wood will have even more appeal.

Jin is obviously then a good method of disguising any major surgery on conversion of evergreen nursery stock into Bonsai. Whitened areas on the trunk can also add greatly to the charm of a tree and occur naturally where trees are forced to endure harsh conditions.

The best season for jin or sabimiki on an evergreen is over winter but the subject must have cold shelter. Frost hitting such areas is often disaster.

Uro or concave carving with deciduous trees is best done in early August onwards. The tree must be shaded afterwards and winter protection given. If carved earlier than August the tree will often check and if done later it will not be active enough to heal properly.

LEAF CUTTING—Trident Maple, Elm, Zelkova only.

This is the means of inducing two seasons' growth in one. Finer twig growth results, the second set of leaves is smaller and autumn colour is better.

When the leaves are leather-hard (around May/July) cut the leaves off with sharp scissors. Leave the petiole, or leaf-stalk, to nourish the plant. New leaves will appear in about 3 weeks.

Precede the process by extra feeding and continue while and after new leaves are formed. DO NOT carry out leaf cutting on weak, newly potted or re-potted trees; or, on weakened portions of strong trees. Trees must be strong.

GROOMING

This is the process whereby in conjunction with wiring, the refined shapes of Bonsai are attained and maintained. A little lengthening of the shoots is desirable in the formative stages as these take better both to pruning and to wiring. Grooming really means pruning for character. Check each twig carefully and prune so that a change of angle results or so that buds will

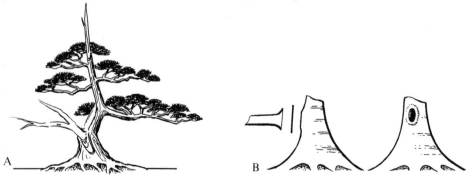

Scar techniques:
A Evergreens Jin. Conversion of tip and lower branch to decorative silver areas
B Deciduous trees. Conversion of scar on large branch removal to decorate hollow or Uro

56

be encouraged to break further along branch lines. Remove twigs that are overcrowded. Study each plane and prune so that the periphery densens and thereby neatens. Always remove ragged undergrowth and base shoots from trained branches. From time to time branches should be thinned out and the negative areas between foliage masses considered. These negative shapes are as artistic and important to the design as the structure itself. They also serve the utility function of admitting light and air to every portion of the tree. A tree with foliage that is too dense is boring visually and in danger of branch shedding due to lack of light and disease or insect attack due to poor ventilation. Trimming also exposes the framework of the tree and successive grooming will reveal the angled twigs thus achieved and contribute charm and age to the result. Lastly, grooming helps maintain the vigour index. Twig thinning should be greater in the upper reaches of the tree, particularly the apex. This is based on the simple fact that every trunk thickens in relation to the branch load and therefore every branch to the twig weight. Lower branches should be allowed as full a spread as possible in keeping with the design and the head kept simplified as possible. Neglected Bonsai and trees collected in nature often show top dominance and weakened lower areas.

WIRING

Wiring is the mechanical means to achieve a radical change of trunk pattern or a realignment of foliage masses. Without grooming, wiring will not achieve very much. After initial trunk bending allow the tree a rest of some weeks before further refinement if extensive. It is good practice for the novice to wire a little loosely. Rapid increases in trunk and branch caliper will scar the tree badly—watch for these increases in late summer—and looser wire obviously presents less hazard. Also in the first stages, a tree wired loosely is not so easily cracked but be cautious. Do not try to do everything in one go. It is better to give trunk and main branches their main directions first and to come back later when the tree has obviously recovered and is growing happily. Then ensure that same season subsidiary wiring is gentle. Everything so far is pointing to the establishment of a successful unfolding design and careless subsidiary wiring can check the tree badly. Current year growth can be retarded and limbs even lost completely. Once bent, do no contra-bend, this ruptures tissues badly. Always secure the wire end in the soil for trunk coiling and around a neighbouring branch in limb coiling. Gently flex-test the limb or trunk with fingers or hands and match the wire gauge in resistance feel. Make major bends first and then leave minor areas if there are many of these till later. Subjects such as Maples or Apricots which can react badly with bare wire should be shaped either with plastic covered wire or wire coiled with masking tape. New shoots whilst soft are always best shaped with covered wire.

Sometimes when a tree is very small or very brittle it is shaped by guying down. This is called suspended wiring. Cherries, which resent wire, are best trained by this method. A piece of softening material such as rubber or plastic tubing material should be wrapped around both friction areas. Wires are then secured from the limb to the trunk with enough tension to give the desired bend. If the limb is particularly brittle, consider making a turnbuckle by means of a loop in the centre of the taut wire which can thus be tightened gradually over a month or two, gently achieving the completed bend.

Other methods comprise the use of clamps and various formers for training stout trunks and branches. The safest former for the beginner to use is a section of heavy gauge galvanized wire that is shaped to the projected trunk pattern. This is tied to the trunk top and bottom and successive ties are made at major bends. If this is carefully done it has a lot to commend it as a shaping aid for those who still feel worried over wiring. Important points to remember are the cushioning of friction areas and the frequent checking for constriction at the points. Major branches may also be trained in this way.

'Setting' of any trunk or branch in position will vary with the species and age of the subject but is usually anywhere from a month to three months for young deciduous subjects and from one month to a year or more for evergreens.

Finally, do not wire newly repotted trees or trees in their first potted year. Wire currently in use is usually solid copper in 8-22 gauge. This can be heated/annealed when about to be used for greater elasticity. A lighted ball of newspapers and five minutes of such gentle heating is usually enough. Greater heat makes the wire brittle. Let the wire cool normally. Currently, copper anodized aluminium wire is in use in Japan. This is very pliable and yet keeps the line easily and would seem to be the best wire to date. Other wires are the single core type sheathed in plastic. Do not use galvanized wire; it rusts and is hard to remove.

AGING
This is the use of a variety of techniques to create apparent age where the material is young. A lot of this will already have been mentioned but a list will clarify the purpose of each technique and help the selection for specific effect.

TRUNK SHAPE
Where young trunks grow straight and strong, so old trees adjust and realign with the passage of years. With the exception of Formal Upright styles therefore, the more changes of angle, however minute, the greater the feeling of age in the trunk. These angles, it is stressed, do not have to be distorted—very often the deviation from the straight of 6mm/$\frac{1}{4}$in is enough to add charm to an otherwise visually boring line. In general, straight lines indicate young growth, which develop in one year, so you should aim for at least one change of direction in every 10cm/4in of vertical growth (unless it constitutes part of a major bend) to evoke character and the feeling of time. Often simple pruning above a pair of buds so that the trunk is forced to realign is enough to give the required kink. Sometimes deep pruning back to a fork will radically change an uninteresting trunk area. The new leader being formed from one of the fork laterals creates a natural-looking change of plane. Always clean out fork cuts leaving a concave contour for inconspicuous healing.

Wiring and its variants are the obvious way to create major trunk designs, or redesigns, and if used with the kink pruning method, the ensuing blend of curve and straight line gives a wonderfully diverse and interesting form. A little cold-blooded planning is all that is required and the patience to realise the programme may take some years to complete. Remember too, apart from the upright styles, a tree planted at an angle evokes age. Saplings are usually vertical.

TRUNK TEXTURE

This varies according to species and perhaps that chosen for the mood which the design indicates. For instance, a rough-barked, chunky Pine may be visualised growing over a stone or as a cascade raking downwards, or again a grove of smooth-trunked Beech might be seen growing on a knoll. Such textures can be programmed to an extent. In the case of the Beech and such species which are gentle in feeling, meticulous attention should be paid to the early removal of unnecessary shoots lest their subsequent woody growth leaves scars on pruning. Any heavy branch removal should be carried out so only carved concave areas are left which heal flat, or if very large, the Uro hollow should be left. Good watering and feeding methods are most important to encourage the trunks to become smooth and rounded.

ROOTAGE

Together with trunk shape and texture, the roots complete the natural attitude or posture of good Bonsai. Ideally the roots should strike into the ground with force enough to justify the trunk caliper. The radial spread too is of great importance. Early attention to repotting methods now repay the time spent. The surface roots by the age of 3-4 years should clearly dominate and command a ridged, strong appearance. They will assume the appearance of trunk bark if well exposed, so keep mosses well trimmed away from major root lines.

With trunks that are upright a four-directional spread contributes greatly to the power of the tree. With those trees that slant from the base, great care should be taken to surface heavy roots on the inside face of the angle. The rake line is always satisfactory, as the higher side of the trunk pulls up and emphasizes that side of the system. When the inner angle roots are lifted, the Bonsai is visually stablized and formation looks strong—like a lion's claw.

Maples will produce a web-like system of major surface roots if left comparatively undisturbed when repotting. This means removing small roots that stem directly from the trunk and clutter major root lines, and wash old soil away between major roots, so new soil can feed them without competition. The results of these techniques is the generation of great girth in the major surface roots which in time meet and coalesce completely. The name for this huge four-directional plate is the table-top, and it is probably the most charming formation for a single maple planting.

BRANCHING
This should be diverse in form, short in internodal length and in the case of all trees (except the upright and broom styles) should weep slightly with upturned terminals. Old trees, it will be noted, tend to be flattish or round crowned. Branching tends to gently fall away from this area until the base where bottom lines are often quite raked. A well grown Oak, Beech or Chestnut often displays such giant old lower limbs. These curve down except for the tips. Young trees on the other hand are nearly always vigorously conical in their habit. Bear this in mind and aging the framework will be greatly simplified.

SCAR AREAS
The techniques of jin, sabamiki and Uro, apart from their prime function, can often be considered as design extensions. A tastefully branched conifer that still looks a bit dull can often be transformed into a dramatic and older form by bark stripping areas of trunk and branches. By extensive top jin, tall seedlings can appear as lightning-scarred old trees. When areas of the trunk are very exposed, this style of tree is often called Driftwood.

REPOTTING
Usually carried out at Spring bud-swelling time. This is the all-important process necessary to maintain the health of the tree in a restricted environment. The older portions of the root ball are removed, space thus being provided for the production of new ciliary or feeder roots to absorb the fresh nutrients provided at this time and with feeding. This coincides with a shortening and trimming of the branch system to keep a balance. This should not be neglected. The whole tree's metabolism is rejuvenated and a happy tree with an aged trunk and lively vigorous branching results.

1 *Ease the tree from the pot.* The root ball may sometimes stick—if so take a knife and cut along the wall of the pot.

2 *Cleanse the roots.* Make a mark on the soil $\frac{1}{3}$ of the way across the width of the root ball and with a stick gently remove the outer $\frac{1}{3}$ of soil with an outward motion. This may take some time but be patient; unravel long roots carefully. Remove about $\frac{1}{3}$ or less of the soil from the base. Cut $\frac{1}{2}$ of the exposed root away with clean, sharp scissors that do not crush the roots. Look for older, darker roots and shorten these also but make this old root cutting no more than 20% at any single repotting. Cut the roots of Pines less. Spread and even the root mass. This makes for uniform top development. Clean the container.

3 *Tying the tree.* Pass covered wires through the drainage holes which should be long enough to cross and tie over the root ball. Lay the ends over the rim of the pot.

4 *Locating the tree.* Place crocking over drainage holes: plastic net or perforated zinc are often used. Add 1·3/$\frac{1}{2}$in layer of coarse sand for drainage and layer of relevant soil mix for species. Position tree on soil. Changes of posture may be carried out if desired by building up the soil to tilt the Bonsai or shaving the bottom of the root ball at an angle. Make sure the tree is not too high or too low in the container. The former makes for an awkwardly emphasized root nucleus, the latter loses the advantage of main surface roots which are so valuable in suggesting age. Draw the wires over the root mass and tie together, not tightly, but enough to steady the tree until it settles.

5 *Finishing the soil.* Add soil mix around the roots, working it in with fingers and sometimes a stick, if very lightly held, (like a pencil) to get rid of air pockets. Continue this process until the tree feels fairly stable. Add soil up to 1·3cm/$\frac{1}{2}$in or rim of container. Never at any time apply excessive pressure even if it makes you feel like a Bonsai master—roots are easily damaged. Level surface soil and add pieces of moss around the trunk base between the main roots. These will probably need refirming after watering.

6 *Water.* Water with a fine spray till water trickles from drainage holes, then place the Bonsai in a shady spot (no wind, sun or rain) for two weeks. Then gradually allow it more light and according to its species, restore it to its usual location. The second watering is usually due after a week but

observe the soil carefully around the trunk for signs of dryness inside that period.

7 *Feeding*. For safety, delay feeding for six weeks to two months after repotting.

8 *Training*. Provided nothing major is attempted light trimming may be carried out in the normal way if the tree grows vigorously after repotting. Do not wire in the year of repotting.

All Bonsai should be rotated weekly for even sunlight exposure. Failure to observe this can induce lop-sided growth or even the death of branches. Always sterilize tools prior to use with methyl alcohol.

1 *Left* Pot too small for spread. Lines cluttered
2 *Right* Tree after pruning, wiring and overdense foliage removal

1   2

3

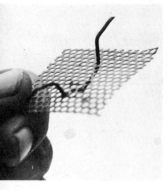

4

5

6

7

8

3   Screen net prepared showing wire U with ends formed to simulate pot location
4   Tie strings passed through drainage holes and located net screens
5   Strings and drainage course
6   Root mass showing areas of beneficial white mould – Mycelium – which grows in association with healthy Pine roots. Note heavy base roots
7   Combed out root mass. Heavy roots now pendant
8   Root mass after initial 'chop'

9 Combing out prior to evening root mass
10 Evening root mass
11 Root mass prior to finger teasing for radial placement
12 Root mass spread. Tree located prior to tying in and soil finishing
13 Watering in – soil first – with fine rose
14 Finished result. Tree tied in and featuring newly surfaced radial root system.
Note suspension hook left free. Future foliage pads will be built on established
'herringbone'. Negative areas must be carefully preserved to prevent filled in
appearance of first photograph

15   16   17

15   Pomegranate 25 years. Main lines masked by 'ingrowths' rising shoots and those breaking across

16   After shot of same tree. Basic lines re-established. Some emerging tips are left for projected branch formation. Branches are being permitted a controlled extension of 2.5cm/1in annually

17   English Yew. Triple trunk style. Age 20 yrs. Ht. 80cm/32in. Pot: 55cm/22in.

20   'Soft' tip removal of Chinese Juniper shoot with thumb and forefinger to induce side growths.

21   'Hard' shoot removal on Black Pine with scissors to produce neat secondary shoots

22   Leaf cutting Trident Maple. Leaf stalks are retained. Compare with foliage of Raft Style Trident

20   21   22

18   Alberta Spruce. Group style. Age 12-15 yrs. Ht. 30cm/12in. Pot: 90cm/36in. Irregular grey Fibreglass. From Nursery stock. Nuclear arrangement is good but contours and branching tiering need the 'Upright style treatment' to create negative areas and simplify lines.

19   Japanese Red Maple var. Seigen. Informal style. Age 90 yrs. Ht. 67.5cm/27in. Pot: 55cm/22in. Grey burnished Kobeware. Imported tree. Trunk taper, posture branch arrangement and root flair are good. Note domed foliage pads. Will be repotted into larger pot in Spring 1978

9   SOIL

Make sure this is open and spongy in texture. A mixture of grit, peat and loam will provide an excellent growth medium for virtually all species. Ensure that this is well-sieved and feel for sponginess of texture by gripping random handfuls when mixing. All materials should be dry. The soil is the vehicle that enables the ramified root system to breathe and expand freely. If the soil is sound, then root activity is rapid and this happy state of affairs is reflected in top growth which is even and vigorous. If however the soil is ill-drained and heavy, there will be no ventilation and the root system will drown and rot. Such soil, in Bonsai slang, is known as the 'death mix' and rightly so! Do not therefore use excessively loamy soils for any Bonsai even if this saves labour in watering—the tree always suffers and will ultimately die.

10 POTS AND CONTAINERS

POTS

Open ground, growth box or finished tree container all have their function. Never prematurely pot any trees. The temptation to stick you first batch of trees in pots is great but every tree has its 'vigour point' and this is best obtained by a rest period of free growth after shaping sometimes for a period of years. The framework is encouraged to thicken and the trunk expands freely giving an aged look that the potted tree cannot achieve in anything like the same period. When the 'vigour point' is reached, the tree will be developing at a tremendous rate and this stage is therefore clearly recognizable. It is good practice to combine growth box and open ground culture alternately for ease of refinement. The final pot is one that will suit and complement the completed tree shape. In general, a relationship of 20% pot to 80% tree is followed for graceful and non-chunky trees. For heavy trunked or low spreading trees a combination of 40% pot to 60% tree is favoured. Desirable pot characteristics are a porous or semi-porous body with ample drainage holes. Do not buy warped Bonsai pots with 'puddles' in the base in which water can collect. Avoid internally glazed pots. A porous body breathes and helps keep the soil sweet and a dark colour absorbs solar heat readily and will assist in promoting root growth. An unglazed pot will have a 'tooth' on which fresh root tops can bind and thus help stabilize the tree.

CONTAINERS
Colours

Earth colours are best for all plants as they do not distract the eye. They represent the earth. They should be chosen for conifers. Off-white, blue, yellow, green and purple may be used as a contrast value to the flowering and fruiting species, provided nothing too glaring is used. Understatement is the keynote.

Opposite top Scots Pine (60 years)

Opposite bottom Trident Maple over stone (12 years)

68

Shape

Basically: oval, rectangle, round and hexagonal. There are various composite shapes. Try to make the chosen pot echo or complement the design of the tree without distracting the eye.

Texture

Always unglazed inside. Matt or rough finished pots look well with conifers. Even with glazed containers try to avoid too shiny a finish—if present, a little emery powder works wonders.

11 WATERING

It is said that watering of Bonsai is tricky. This is true to the extent that many factors come into play. The basic fact is that a Bonsai needs enough water present in the soil to preserve the moisture balance throughout the system and this normally means a constantly and consistently moist soil. Use of the recommended well drained soil will greatly aid this condition and yet retain enough air through the structure to prevent the death mix syndrome. With the knowledge of sound soil structure and knowing that it must remain moist, regulating the water given can inhibit the production of too long nodes. The tree and its placement must be studied in relation to local environmental conditions and once familiar with these, water should be given at the rate to maintain soil moisture and no more. An elevated shelf assists in preventing overgrowth and will be discussed under 'Placement'.

Trees in small pots will require extra attention and all trees will benefit from leaf spray after sunset on hot or particularly windy days. Exact knowledge of local conditions will dictate frequency of watering but as a general rule once or twice daily in spring/summer and every other day or quite possibly less during autumn/winter. Control of watering is comparatively easy during the growing season but is deceptive during dormancy. The forefinger and thumb test is best during dormancy—pinch up a small amount and roll it—if it is oozy, ease off the water—if it just clings, water is perfect and if it

Opposite Japanese White Pine (200-300 years)

powders, re-read this section! Those unfortunate enough to live in areas of high water chlorination will occasionally experience trouble with acid loving subjects such as Azaleas. This problem can be largely overcome by the use of additional leaf mould (well sieved!) in the basic soil mix and in the storage of water before use for a day or so.

Watering should be carried out using a hose or can with a fine nozzle. Regard the fall as rain and do not disturb the soil. First apply to the soil till water drips steadily from the drainage holes of the pot, then sprinkle the tree itself. Wait for fifteen minutes and repeat, and this secondary application will ensure even saturation. It is not always necessary to give such a heavy second application. Do not allow water on foliage during hot sun as this causes burning.

12 FEEDING

All Bonsai must be fed regularly throughout the growing season. Trees which are not fed adequately are miserably coloured and próne to die-back and disease. It is asking a lot of a tree confined to a restricted environment to maintain its health when subject to pruning and styling regimes, and feed plays a key role in the vigour of each Bonsai. This sounds obvious enough but it is surprising how often even experienced growers will seriously underfeed their trees. Feeding in Bonsai is usually regarded from the standpoint of maintaining specimen trees. These will generally require less feed than developing trees. The problem that exists is where the accepted feeding rate is applied to all trees thereby denying young trees their full potential.

A liquid feed is usually the best and those of foliar type are even more useful in their action. The feed is absorbed through the system rapidly and a more even reaction to the feed is noticeable. The season for feeding varies with the species but normally begins in March and finishes in October. With all deciduous species the best period to begin feeding is when bud activity begins and new leaves show as coloured dots. Repeat feed twice a week for two weeks and then once every ten days till September. Those species grown for flower and fruit should not be fed while in flower and those that set fruit, such as Crab Apples, should not be fed between flower till embryo fruit has reached 1.3cm/½in size. Feeding during this time causes fruits to drop. Flowering and fruiting species should also have the feed supplemented with bone meal given later in the season— end of July onwards once a month. Pines and Conifers fed late—September and October—will thicken as a result. It is a good practice to feed Pines from January onwards, monthly, till regular feeding schedules begin in March. Conifers are slightly root active during dormancy and such feeds will maintain the health and colour of Pines and build reserves of strength. Conifers should be fed fortnightly from March to September. Deciduous subjects should not be fed between October and March as feed can cause root decay. Just be careful to feed as soon as bud activity starts.

Developing trees should be fed at the mentioned rate but older more finished Bonsai require only enough food to maintain balanced vigour throughout the tree. This normally means a good monthly feed but trees vary and even old ones many need a supplementary feed if bad foliage colour or sluggish reactions appear overall or in parts of the Bonsai. Older Bonsai sometimes suffer from undernourishment in an abortive effort by their owners to preserve nicely styled shapes or even worse, to control foliage texture by witholding feed. This is always a bad policy as trees so weakened often shed the very limbs the owner seeks to preserve in pristine condition.

13 PLACEMENT

Potted Bonsai should be placed at viewing height on elevated shelving. Normal viewing height is considered to be with the midway point on the trunk at eye level. This may be found too high for practical maintenance and tentative set-ups may be tried out first. The shelving should be simple and quiet in colour. Larger Bonsai sit better visually on heavy timber but small trees should have something lighter. The shelving should be gapped or slotted to facilitate ventilation. Sun exposure is vital for health and in conjunction with ventilation makes for neat foliage texture. In the UK one has seldom to worry over excessive light even at midday, but certain subjects benefit from light shading such as Yew and Cryptomeria. This can easily be rigged up using netting or spaced lathing but is not essential for the health of any tree in the UK. All trees have a range of pigmentation present in the foliage and those in full sun will be towards the yellow in appearance. Neither is 'correct' for Bonsai, but is a matter of individual preference.

Bonsai should be placed far enough apart to be enjoyed in isolation and the erection of some background might be considered. This is not vital but is done if existing conditions provide too confusing a background or if prevailing winds are a nuisance. Larch lap fencing for instance makes a pleasant visual termination but beware of placing this or any background too close to the shelving as you immediately get problems from reflected heat. The use of backgrounds or overhead screening as a wind baffle is sensible if winds are a problem but normally trees are stronger if allowed moderate wind exposure.

Newly potted Bonsai or those with slightly unstable designs, such as Cascades or Windswept should be secured to the shelving with strings that pass over the soil complete and round the bench.

Trees may be brought indoors for short viewing periods, normally not for more than 1-2 days. If they are displayed indoors during cold weather, allow the Bonsai the same period in which to cool off (a shed or outhouse is ideal) before returning to external temperatures.

Whilst indoors, spray the foliage to maintain humidity and do not place the tree on the TV or in a room where central heating is going full blast. Bonsai must live outdoors.

14   DISEASES

ROOT ROT
Often caused by overwatering a newly potted or repotted tree. With the use of the recommended soil mixture this should not

be a great danger. The witholding of regular watering schedules until roots have established is the prime rule. The tree should be watered thoroughly first and then a light misting on the foliage daily will help. Do not water the soil again until drying is definitely evident. The soil will settle a little with watering and the thing to avoid at all costs is total settlement of soil before the roots can penetrate. Normal watering should be established slowly, say over 2-3 weeks.

The other major causes of root rot are our old friend the death mix—heavy soil that denies air penetration; premature feeding which adversely affects the roots at a time when feeder roots are minimal, and the most difficult cause to determine— rot through underwatering. The last often happens during dormancy where the soil appears moist but drying winds are removing foliage moisture at a greater rate than can be coped with by the drying roots. The tree loses it balance of moisture and dessication of twigs and trunk follows. This is apparent in thin fissures that appear in the bark in parallel with the shape of the limb. If this is diagnosed in the spring when growth has failed to start (and this applies to overwatered trees too) take a tree out of the pot and prepare a temporary container such as a wooden box. Branching should be pruned back a little to help preserve moisture balance. Mix together coarse sand and leaf mould, say about 3 to 1, or more of sand if the leaf mould is bulky. Plant the tree in this mixture and thereafter treat it as a gigantic cutting, ie mist foliage twice a day and after initial soil watering, hold back and check for moistness before re-watering. Shade the tree. Spray foliage with systemic fungicide fortnightly and a little vitamin B_1 transplant solution is also an aid applied to the root—single application only. Thereafter time will tell. If the damage is not too severe, the chances of saving even an old tree are about 60-40 in favour if the trouble is dealt with promptly.

NEMATODES

These are wart-like swellings which appear on the roots of certain species mainly the Rosaceae such as Quince and Cotoneaster. The top symptoms are flagging growth and general tiredness in growth performance. Nematodes should be checked for at spring repotting time or in August/September in the case of Quince and Cotoneaster. which must have post-transplant winter care. Taking a sharp knife, the nematodes should be sliced off and a prophylactic applied—systemic fungicide sprayed directly on the cut is generally effective. Plant the trees in a temporary container with as little further root disturbance as possible. Water with restraint and apply fungicide fortnightly for a month to 6 weeks.

MILDEW
Mildew is a disease that usually strikes when ventilation is poor and temperatures are high—the ensuing humidity provides a perfect condition for mildew and virus conditions. Mildew usually appears as discoloured hairy areas on any part of the tree and deciduous species are usually worst effected. Treatment consists of the removal of all affected foliage and some thinning of foliage masses generally. Check ventilation and if placement is the problem a sunnier spot should be found where the air moves freely. The thinning will help if the tree has for any reason to remain in situ. Burn all infected debris and clean soil surface meticulously of any trash. Spray with either weak Bordeaux mixture of systemic fungicide. Two such sprays are usually sufficient. Trident Maples for example, with their dense foliage, are often subject to such attacks and the trouble is this case is often viral. It appears that early aphid attacks in the spring can cause leaf spotting disease and these are very long lasting once they got a hold. Therefore it is good practice to routinely spray for aphids very early in the season and to follow this after a week or so with fungicide. Heavy soil or overwatering will also cause this appearance.

There is another main cause of leaf discolouration in conifers, so I have included it under the Mildew heading because superficially the damage appears similar. This damage is the after effects of an attack by red spider mites usually in early spring/summer when the season is very dry. The appearance is sad and there is a lot of leaf-browning either ringing the section of leaf or causing large areas of browning through the foliage mass. Curiously, current foliage seldom falls despite the alarming dead look and will usually recover. Cure and/or prevention of red spider attack consists of routine spraying with malathion from early spring, say monthly. As dryness appears to encourage the mites, then obviously leaf spraying with water is sensible. Spruce, Pine and Chinese Juniper are all prone to red spider, so be vigilant. If damage occurs, red spider can be discovered by holding white paper under the affected foliage. When tapped, the foliage will yield a shower of minute red insects like a dusting of Cayenne pepper.

15 PESTS

All Bonsai are subject to attacks by insects but for the most part these are easily kept in check by spraying with appropriate solutions.

APHIDS

These usually appear with the new growth and in conjunction with ants. Therefore if some provision is made to eliminate the ants, the aphids become more controllable. An alternative regime of spraying first with a systemic and then with Malathion or Pyrethrum a fortnight later will usually keep the aphids down.

MEALY BUGS/WOOLLY APHIDS

The insects usually infest Pines but Beech and Apples are sometimes affected. Treat as for aphids, but after 48 hours spray with a strong water jet to remove the dead insects which adhere and look like cotton wool. Subsequent attacks are thus easily spotted. Individual painting with methylated spirits of infected areas is effective when the attack is severe.

SCALE

These look like small pods or blimps adhering to trunk and branches and may be destroyed by hand or by spraying with an emulsion spray.

CATERPILLARS

Random shoot damage on any plant or succulent leaves with great areas missing are usually signs of these larvae. Once again, if the attack is extensive, a quick dose of systemic spray will clear it up but usually there are only one or two culprits.

EARTHWORMS AND ROOT APHIDS

The former does not do great damage other than to create holes in the root mass which can lead to root problems. Usually as Bonsai are displayed on shelves this invasion will not occur. If present, they are best removed at repotting time. Root aphids can largely be discouraged with the use of systemics if their presence is suspected during the growing season. A general flagging of the tree, particularly Pines, is a good indication of root aphid. At repotting time, check the root mass carefully and spray systemic directly on to the roots. It is easy to confuse the white mould beneficial to the Pines with the white insects, so inspect carefully. If necessary, use a magnifying glass. The mould will appear as a contiguous white frill. As a useful cross-check, the beneficial white mould, called mycelium, will be recognized, particularly in autumn by its highly fungoid/resinous smell.

16 TOOLS

Shears are used for root pruning and branch trimming. These should have long fine tipped blades. Secateurs are used for heavy pruning or a light saw. Wire cutters of the scissor type are useful. A revolving stand is useful for turning the tree in wiring and training. Tools should be kept clean and sharp. Methyl alcohol should be used for sterilisation. Never let tools become rusty. Japanese tools are available in the UK but English substitutes are as good.

17 BONSAI DATA

CHINESE JUNIPER
Type of tree and main features
Fine textured evergreen. Accent on contours of foliage pads.

Best Styles
Informal – driftwood – cascade and semi-cascade – gnarled – twin or triple trunk – stone clasped.

Repotting Season

Ideally March/April, but providing aftercare and shade are given any time during growing season. Every 2 years. Up to 5 years for older trees.

Soil Mix

6 parts John Innes No. 2
4 parts coarse sand
Provide good drainage and do not compress soil too much.

Watering

Ample watering and foliage mist.

Feeding

Fortnightly from March to October. Use a nitrogen feed for rich colour.

Pruning/Grooming

Feeding encourages plumose foliage sprays that must be finger pinched. Use the soft part of thumb and forefinger and pinch off when tip growth is long enough. This spurs side shooting which must also be tipped. Do not pinch too deeply as this causes browning, die-back and gorse-like juvenile growth to appear. Grooming: cleaning out relaxed shoots that break trained lines and any shoots in branched forks.

Wire Shaping

Winter. Emphasise the pads of foliage by spreading the mass created by pruning. Domed foliage pads are favoured for this Juniper, so really employ the suggested herringbone base for the mass to rest upon. Make every branch express three dimensional depth.

Placement

Good light is essential but sun can burn in sunny months so have light shade handy.

Winter Placement

Chinese Juniper is hardy but direct frost will turn foliage a ghastly grey brown so light shelter is best.

Pests and Diseases
Red Spider – Malathion. Rust disease – Systemic fungicide.

Container
An elegant container on the deep side is best.

Trees given largely the same treatment

NEEDLE JUNIPER – Prune for light and air penetration.
Lower limbs are otherwise endangered.

SAWARA CYPRESS – HINOKI CYPRESS – CRYPTOMERIA – SPRUCE
Points of difference: nip off extensions on foliage frills with both Cypress. Finger pinch Cryptomeria when growths are 1.25cm/$\frac{1}{2}$in long. Ample water and mist. Spruce are pinched as growth comes out, working gradually over the tree. Allow shoots 2.5cm/1in growth before finger pruning.

JAPANESE BLACK PINE
Type of tree and main features
Needled evergreen. Two needles to a sheath. Rough bark and erect dark needles.

Best Styles
All bar Besom.

Repotting Season
March/April or August, if aftercare over Winter can be provided. 2-5 years according to age.

Soil Mix
3 parts John Innes No. 2
3 parts leaf mould
5 parts coarse sand
Check texture carefully – no fine particles.

Watering
Keep moist and mist foliage. During shoot growth restrained use of water can help needle tidiness.

Feeding
Monthly January – October.

Pruning/Grooming
Pinch off overgrown shoots completely when needles just start to appear as points in the shoot wall. Continue removing overlong primary shoots as they are produced and they will be replaced by numerous secondary shoots. The secondary shoots will have neat foliage and every branch plane will soon appear dense. Groom out overcrowded areas of foliage and keep underlines meticulously free of old and hanging needles.

Wire Shaping
Autumn/winter. Spread side shoots using herringbone. Elevate each tip for neater periphery.

Placement
Full sun.

Winter Placement
Frost protection for the sake of needle colour.

Pests and Diseases
Mealy Bugs, Woolly Aphids, Red Spider are the most common. Pyrethrum, Malathion and systemic insecticide.

Container
Traditionally simple oval or rectangular forms of medium or greater depth are used.

Trees given largely the same treatment:

BLACK PINE variety: Corticata, varies from the type in Pruning treatment. Shoots are normally pinched lightly, half to one-third being taken. Branch tips are pruned once every other year.

SCOTS PINE – MUGO PINE – PITCH PINE

JAPANESE WHITE PINE
Type of tree and main features
Needles evergreen. Five needles to a sheath. Silver appearance due to white stomatic band down each leaf.

Best Styles
All bar Besom.

Repotting Season
March/April or August, if aftercare over winter can be provided. 2-5 years according to age.

Soil Mix
2 parts John Innes No. 2
3 parts leaf mould
5 parts coarse sand

Watering
> **As for Black Pine**

Feeding

Pruning/Grooming
Pinch shoots lightly, taking no more than half to one-third of each. Basal shoots and some latent buds should appear. Denser budding can further be encouraged by tip pruning each branch during August of every other year.
Grooming: old foliage and dense areas should be removed/thinned in August/September. Groom each branch meticulously as for Black Pine.

Wire Shaping

Placement

Winter Placement > **As for Black Pine**

Pests and Diseases

Container

LARCH

Type of tree and main features

Deciduous conifer. Bright green 'star' foliage in spring and gold autumn colour. Interesting branch structure and rough bark in aging specimens.

Best Styles

Upright single trunk – Informal. Experiment with other styles except Besom.

Repotting Season

March/April as buds show first green. Every two years. Less often for older specimens. Can be touchy after root disturbance so watch watering carefully.

Soil Mix

3 parts John Innes No. 2
3 parts leaf mould
4 parts coarse sand
Good drainage course.

Watering

After 'settling in' period in repotting years, give abundantly.

Feeding

Fortnightly March – October.

Pruning/Grooming

Growing season: pinch back soft shoots when latent buds are apparent. Select bud pointing in desired growth direction and pinch above this – not too close.

Autumn: prune back branch tips with scissors for dense budding in the following year. Remove any flimsy looking wayward shoots. Aim for a chunky pollarded appearance along each branch.

Wire Shaping

Autumn/winter. Suspended wiring and loose coiling are safest due to fragile bark.

Placement
Full sun.

Winter Placement
Light frost protection but not essential.

Pests and Diseases
Mostly free.

Container
Traditionally oval or rectangular forms of medium or greater depth are used, i.e. 6.5cm/2½in – 9cm/3½in.

CHINESE ELM
Type of tree and main features
Deciduous, broadleaved. Old bark is rough like Scots Pine or smooth according to variety. Dense twigs.

Best Styles
Informal – besom – group – clasped to stone.

Repotting Season
March. Every other year, say, up to 10 years and then by root ball observation.

Soil Mix
6 parts John Innes No. 2
3 parts leaf mould
1 part coarse sand
Check for sponginess of texture. Sift well.

Watering
Once a day or more during hot spells. Never let soil get dry as young inner leaves will die.

Feeding
When first buds open feed weekly for a month then fortnightly till September.

Pruning/Grooming

The tree is very strong and should be kept well pinched back. Reduce shoots to 2 sets of leaves over the mass and back to 1 set of leaves at the apex.

Grooming: consider each branch plane and clean underlines first. Work up from the 'herringbone' and remove inner growths so the framework of twigs can be seen supporting each pad. Always remove larger leaves to encourage finer texture.

Wire Shaping

Mid-summer. Covered wires or suspended wiring.

Placement

Beware of total exposure to sun and wind – *light* shade is best.

Winter Placement

Light frost protection or fine twigs will be lost in hard winters.

Pests and Diseases

Aphids – Pyrethrum.

Container

Traditionally, an oval or rectangular form which may be glazed.

Trees given largely the same treatment:

ZELKOVA – HACKBERRY – HORNBEAM – BEECH – BIRCH

Points of difference: with regard to the latter four, only large leaves are removed and pinching is lighter.

JAPANESE MAPLE

Type of tree and main features

Deciduous, broadleaved. Five-lobed leaf and dense growth habit. Older trees have silvery bark. Autumn colour is usually red.

Best Styles

Informal – group – clasped to stone.

Repotting Season
Mid-March. Every other year, say, up to 10 years and then by root ball observation.

Soil Mix
5 parts John Innes No. 2
5 parts coarse sand
Check soil texture. Sift well. Drainage course is vital.

Watering
Once a day or more during hot spells. Evening mist is beneficial.

Feeding
When first buds open feed weekly for a month then fortnightly till September.

Pruning/Grooming
Trim back to 1–2 pairs of leaves after shoots have extended some little way. Premature pinching often causes new shoots to wither.
Grooming: as for Chinese Elm. Leaf cutting on trees up to 15 years only.

Wire Shaping
May/June. Limbs are brittle. Covered wires.

Placement

Winter Placement

Pests and Diseases

Container

As for Chinese Elm. Treat mildew with Bordeaux mixture or systemic fungicide.

Opposite above Trident Maple–August 1977
Opposite bottom Trident Maple–Winter 1978 (80 years)

Varieties
There are various red leaved forms of Japanese Maple which are very striking but they all need special protection until the leaves feel hard.

TRIDENT MAPLE
Type of tree and main features
Deciduous, broadleaved. Three-lobbed leaf and dense growth habit. Older trees have flaking bark which reveals reddish underbark. Root structure is powerful. Autumn colour is usually red.

Best Styles
Informal – group – clasped to stone.

Repotting Season
Mid-March then as for Japanese Maple.

Soil Mix
5 parts John Innes No. 2
5 parts coarse sand
Check soil texture. Sift well. Drainage course is vital.

Watering
Once a day or more during hot spells. Evening misting is beneficial.

Feeding
When buds first open feed weekly for a month than fortnightly until September.

Pruning/Grooming
This tree is almost as strong as Chinese Elm and quickly throws up new shoots that are strongly vertical so, after allowing the usual extension of shoots, pinch back to 1–2 sets of leaves. The adventitious buds that have appeared and produced the vertical shoots should be carefully considered, as

Opposite Chinese Juniper (100 years)

by pruning hard back to a directional bud the foliage pad can often be usefully bulked up. Do not retain too many however as these drain energy from trained areas.

Grooming: is largely as for the Chinese Elm but do pay attention to the vigour cone and thin upper leaf areas to keep a balance. Leaf cutting is carried out in mid-summer, feed well beforehand. Only strong trees.

Wire Shaping
Usually wiring is done during leaf cutting as, with these very dense trees, it is difficult to see the structure. Limbs are brittle. Use covered wire and spread the growth sideways in the herringbone.

Placement
Beware of hot sun and wind but otherwise full sun.

Winter Placement
As for Chinese Elm.

Pests and Diseases
Aphids – Pyrethrum. Scale is also troublesome and should be checked for in winter. Mildew – Bordeaux mixture or systemic fungicide. Destroy scale by hand or spray over winter with oil emulsion.

Container
Medium to shallow containers of particularly oval and rectangular forms are best. Check watering.

CRAB APPLE
Type of tree and main features
Deciduous, broadleaved. Flowers are white, flushed pink in bud. Dark red thumb-nail size fruits.

Best Styles
Informal – leaning – semi-cascade – twin-trunk – clump group.

Repotting Season
March. Every year or by root ball observation.

Soil Mix
4 parts John Innes No. 2
4 parts leaf mould
2 parts coarse sand. Check for sponginess of texture. Sift well.

Watering
Ample water.

Feeding
Generously, weekly till flowering. Allow fruit to swell to thumb-nail size then feed fortnightly till late September.

Pruning/Grooming
Pinch back all new shoots to 2.5cm/1in then do not prune again till autumn. In autumn, trim back any long shoots and neaten twig periphery. Watch out for flower buds when grooming. These are usually bigger than leaf buds. Encourage tight twig clusters.

Wire Shaping
Mid-season. Covered wires.

Placement
Full exposure.

Winter Placement
Light frost protection and protect fruits from birds.

Pests and Diseases
Aphids – Pyrethrum. Mealy bugs – spray overwinter with lime/sulphur in 1-30 water solution and during season with Pyrethrum.

Container
Deep circular, oval or rectangular forms.

JAPANESE APRICOT
Type of tree and main features
Deciduous, broadleaved. Flowers in late winter on bare wood. Flowers may be red, pink or white and there are weeping forms.

Best Styles
Informal – leaning – semi-cascade – driftwood.

Repotting Season
Immediately after flowering.

Soil Mix
6 parts John Innes No. 2
2 parts leaf mould
2 parts coarse sand

Watering
Ample water. Mist flower buds as they open.

Feeding
After flowering, monthly from March–October. Add bone-meal monthly, July–October.

Pruning/Grooming
When flowers fall prune back hard. Let subsequent shoots grow and neaten back in September. If extra growth is wanted finger pinch new shoots but flowering will be effected.

Wire Shaping
Curving downwards promotes flowering. ALWAYS use covered wire.

Placement
Full exposure.

Winter Placement
Light frost protection.

Pests and Diseases
Spray fortnightly with Pyrethrum.

Container
Although the usual oval and rectangles are used it is worth considering more ornate shapes if the tree has strongly decorative features. Glazed ware may be used to great effect.

PYRACANTHA

Type of tree and main features
Deciduous, broadleaved shrub. Flowers white in clusters. Fruits vermilion, heavily borne.

Best Styles
Informal – leaning – cascade and semi-cascade – clasped to stone – twin trunk.

Repotting Season
March. Every two years.

Soil Mix
5 parts John Innes No. 2
5 parts coarse sand

Watering
Ample water. Soil and misting.

Feeding
Generously every week till flowering period. When fruit is fully formed continue feeding fortnightly till October. Supplement feed with bonemeal after fruit is developed.

Pruning/Grooming
On settled branches shorten back new growths to two sets of leaves in late Spring. Cut older wood in early Spring or August. Grooming: trim foliage away from underlines and remove any larger leaves.

Wire Shaping
Try to curve the naturally straight lines of new shoots. Covered wires. Apply wires when shoots have some length but before they harden.

Placement
Full exposure.

Winter Placement
Light frost protection and protect from birds during fruiting season.

Pests and Diseases
Aphids – Pyrethrum. Scale – remove by hand or spray overwinter with oil emulsion.

Container
Deep container is best for moisture conservation. Fancy shapes permissible. Glazed ware may be used.

AZALEA
Type of tree and main features
Evergreen. Flowers in May-July. Grown for shape appeal as well as colour.

Best Styles
Informal – leaning – semi-cascade – twin trunk – clump group – clasped to stone.

Repotting Season
Right after flowers wither. Yearly or as indicated by root mass.

Soil Mix
3 parts loam
3 parts leaf mould
2 parts peat
2 parts coarse sand. Sift well and do not compress soil.

Watering
Ample water. Mist foliage during growing season.

Feeding
Generously, fortnightly till flowering period. After flowering, monthly till September. Supplement with bonemeal.

Pruning/Grooming
Pinch back early growths hard. Secondary growth is pinched more lightly. Do not pinch after mid-summer. In August/September neaten any untidy sprays.
Grooming: clean out any basal shoots from roots or branch lines. Keep branches cleaned underneath. Cut back hard after flowering. Remove old brown foliage in winter. After flower ing 'dead head' withered blooms.

Wire Shaping
After flowering. When shoots have some length and have hardened slightly. Covered wires.

Placement
Full exposure.

Winter Placement
Light frost protection for the sake of foliage colour.

Pests and Diseases
Aphids – spray during growing season with Pyrethrum on a monthly basis.

Container
Deep container is best for moisture conservation. Ovals and rectangular forms are best. Glazed ware may be used.

COTONEASTER
Type of tree and main features
Deciduous flowering shrub. Tiny pink flowers. Bright red berries. Neat foliage. Autumn colour red.

Best Styles
Informal – leaning – cascade – semi-cascade – groups – clasped to stone.

Repotting Season
March. Yearly up to 10 years and then by observation of root ball.

Soil Mix
4 parts John Innes No. 2
4 parts leaf mould
2 parts coarse sand. Test soil texture and sift well. Ample drainage course vital.

Watering
Ample water.

Feeding
Generously weekly till flowering begins. After flowering, weekly till October. Supplement with bonemeal from mid-summer.

Pruning/Grooming
Old branches are pruned in March. Young shoots are normally shortened back to 2 sets of leaves to induce dense twig clusters. Grooming: actually remove some of the herringbone! This shrub has a natural herringbone growth, so break up the regularity for interest. Try to create short twiggy clusters. Clean out surplus twigs meticulously.

Wire Shaping
Mid-summer. Covered wires. Anchor wires on old wood and curve only new shoots. If old wood must be shaped, use suspension ties or clamps. Old wood is brittle.

Placement
Full exposure.

Winter Placement
Light frost protection and protect from birds in fruiting season.

Pests and Diseases
Aphids – Pyrethrum. Scale – destroy by hand or spray over winter with oil emulsion.

Container
Wide choice. Glazed ware may be used. Deep pot for moisture conservation.

JAPANESE QUINCE
Type of tree and main features
Deciduous, broadleaved shrub. Flowers ahead of or with first foliage in late winter/early spring. Flowers red, pink or white.

Best styles
Informal – clump – leaning – semi-cascade – clasped to stone.

Repotting Season
October. Give winter protection. Yearly or every two years.

Soil Mix
6 parts John Innes No. 2
4 parts coarse sand

Watering
Ample water. Mist foliage.

Feeding
After flowering, fortnightly till leaves fall. Supplement with bonemeal from mid-summer.

Pruning/Grooming
Cut back hard after flowering. Allow new shoots 2–3 sets of leaves then pinch tips. Do not prune again till after leaves fall and flower buds can be seen.
Grooming: remove any basal shoots from roots and branch lines. Reduce thin weedy shoots.

Wire Shaping
Mid-season.

Placement
Full exposure.

Winter Placement
Light frost protection. May be brought indoors at flowering time. 'Cool off' plant before returning outside.

Pests and Diseases
Aphids – Pyrethrum. Nematodes – slice off at repotting season and spray with systemic fungicide. Seal cuts with bitumen paint.

Container
Wide variety including glazed ware. Deep forms are best.

POMEGRANATE
Type of tree and main features
Deciduous, broadleaved. Flowers bright red usually but white, pink and yellow forms exist single or double. Fruits seldom form in cool U.K. summers.

Best Styles
Informal – leaning – semi-cascade – twin trunk – cluster group.

Repotting Season
Approximately March. Watch for bud movement and be guided by the tree. Avoid heavy root chopping. Every two years and then up to 10 years by root ball observation.

Soil Mix
5 parts John Innes No. 2
5 parts coarse sand. Ensure good drainage course.

Watering
Ample water. Increase amounts after flowering.

Feeding
Generously, weekly, up to flowering time. Do not use strong feeds and avoid feeding during flowering cycles.

Pruning/Grooming
New growth is shortened back to 2 sets of leaves, whenever it lengthens beyond 3–4 sets of leaves. Shorter, blob-tipped shoots are those carrying embryonic flowers so do not prune these.
Grooming: Pomegranates are very bushy subjects and benefit from thinning out every 2 months during active growth. Heavier branches are cut in mid-summer.

Wire Shaping
Mid-season. Covered wires.

Placement
Full exposure.

Winter Placement
Protect from all frosts and low temperatures. This is a Mediterranean subject.

Pests and Diseases
Aphids – Pyrethrum.

Container
Wide choice either glazed or unglazed. Fancy shapes and simple shapes may be used.

18 CONCLUSION

I hope the basic Bonsai process as I have tried to define it will be found of practical use. The repetitions are included to reinforce areas which are usually neglected. But I do apologize to those finding them tedious.

There are a few points for the newcomer to Bonsai to bear in mind. Knowledge of these will make all the difference to enjoyment of the hobby.

1 Never buy Bonsai from stores having no external display facilities or staffed trained in Bonsai. Be extra cautious at Christmas.

2 Never buy obviously chopped or neglected Bonsai.

3 Do join a good club:
Bonsai Kai of the Japan Society of London;
British Bonsai Association;
Bristol Bonsai Association;
East Midland Bonsai Society, are all recommended. All have sound people who can supply answers to any queries and all have informed and experienced growers of many years standing in their membership. Newcomers approaching these societies are assured of access only to the best in Bonsai.

4 Do visit the Chelsea Flower Show regularly. Here is the greatest concentration of Bonsai on exhibition in Europe. The show provides invaluable help in recognizing what constitutes Bonsai.

5 Never be taken in by cheap advertising or the showmen in Bonsai. Bonsai should not be debased in such a tasteless fashion.
6 Beware the 'Bonsai Tree Seed Kit'! Just planting a seed will not produce a Bonsai. A Bonsai, as you will have gathered is the product of many processes, carefully carried out.

INDEX

Aging 59
Aphids 77
Apricot 9, 48
Apricot, Japanese 91
Azalea 9, 42, 47, 94

Beech 9, 85
Birch 8, 85
Black Pine 81
Bonsai–data 78
  definition of 7
  process 53
  raising from seedling 29
Branching 61

Caterpillars 77
Cedar 7
Chinese Elm 42, 84
Chinese Juniper 78
Containers 70
  colour of 70
  shape 71
  texture 71
Cotoneaster 9, 42, 47, 95
Crab apple 9, 13, 90
Cryptomeria 7, 42, 80
Cuttings 42
Cypress 7, 10, 42
  Hinoki 80
  Sawara 80

Diseases 74

Earthworms 78
Elm 7, 13, 56
Elm, Chinese 42, 84

Feeding 72
Fir 7
Firethorn 9, 42

Grafting 45
Grooming 56

Hackberry 9, 85
Hawthorn 9
Hinoki Cypress 80
Hornbeam 9, 42, 85

Japanese Apricot 91
Japanese Black Pine 80
Japanese Maple 46, 85
Japanese White Pine 82
Jasmine 10, 42
Juniper 9, 42, 46
  Chinese 78
  Needle 80

Laburnum 10
Larch 7, 83
Layering 44
Leaf cutting 56

Maple 7, 10
  Japanese 46, 85
  Senkaki 48
  Trident 7, 42, 56, 89
Mealy bugs 77
Mildew 76
Mountain maple 42
Mugo Pine 81

Needle juniper 80
Nematodes 75
Nursery stock 46

Oak 8

Pests 77
Pine 7, 9
  Black 81

Japanese Black 80
Japanese White 82
Mugo 81
Pitch 81
Scots 81
Placement 73
Pomegranate 98
Pots 70
Pruning 53
Pyracantha 93

Quince 9, 42
   Japanese 96

Repotting 61
Root aphids 78
Root rot 74
Rootage 60

Sawara Cypress 80
Scale 77
Scar areas 61
Scots Pine 81
Seed compost 29
Seed, transplanting of 31
Seedlings, raising from 29
   year 1 29
   year 2 31
   year 3 36
   year 4 40
   year 5 41
Senkaki Maple 48
Soil 67
Spruce 7, 80

Styles
   besom 8,15
   cascade and semi-cascade 10, 19
   clasped to stone 10
   clasped to stone – root over stone 21
   clasped to stone – root confined
      to stone 23
   development of 14
   groups 11, 24
      clump 12
      five and seven trunk 12
      raft style 13, 27
      root connected 13, 28
      triple trunk 12, 25
      twin trunk 11, 25
   informal 17
   informal upright 9
   leaning and windswept 9, 18
   upright single trunk 7, 14

Tools 78
Trees, collecting natural 49
Trident maple 7, 42, 56, 89
Trunk shape 59
Trunk texture 60

Watering 71
Willow 10, 13, 42
Wiring 57
Wisteria 9

Yew 7, 42

Zelkova 7, 8, 42, 56, 85